ANTON EDELMANN
CREATIVE CUISINE

ANTON EDELMANN
CREATIVE CUISINE

FOREWORD BY LEN DEIGHTON

Text in association with Norma MacMillan

Photographs by Gus Filgate

PAVILION

ACKNOWLEDGEMENTS

I would like to thank:

The Directors and Management of The Savoy,
especially Mr Giles Shepard and Mr Herbert Striessnig
for their help and generosity during the writing of this book.

The Chefs in The Savoy kitchens,
especially Derek Rooke and Nana Ntiri-Akuffo.

My assistant, Sophie Petrides, who was of immeasurable help to me.

And Sarah Manser, for all her assistance.

This edition published in Great Britain in 1996 by
PAVILION BOOKS LIMITED
26 Upper Ground, London SE1 9PD

Originally published in hardback in 1993

Text copyright © Anton Edelmann 1993
Foreword copyright © Pluriform Pub. Co. B.V. 1993
Photographs copyright © Gus Filgate 1993

The moral right of the author has been asserted

Contributing editor: Norma MacMillan

Home economist: Linda Tubby

Designed by Bet Ayer

A CIP catalogue record for this book
is available from the British Library.

ISBN 1 85793 991 3

Typeset in American Garamond 10/13$^{1}/_{2}$pt.

Printed and bound in Italy by Graphicom

2 4 6 8 10 9 7 5 3 1

This book may be ordered by post direct from the publisher.
Please contact the Marketing Department. But try your bookshop first.

CONTENTS

CONTENTS

FOREWORD

A year or so ago Anton Edelmann — Maître Chef des Cuisines of the world's most prestigious professional kitchen — told me that he had started work on a book of elegant modern recipes that could be followed by any cook of medium capability in any reasonably equipped kitchen using ingredients that Anton buys in his local high street shops. That is the book you have here: it might be called 'Anton Edelmann at Home' for it reflects a great deal of his taste and experience in half a lifetime spent working with food.

With the fastidious care and attention that he gives to running a kitchen with eighty cooks and purchasing thousands of pounds worth of food per day, he has laboured long and hard to produce a series of foolproof recipes and explain them with a series of 'building blocks' that will enable you to squeeze the most out of your time, efforts and money. As an example, take his amazing orange soufflé which contains virtually no flour and artfully combines quark and beaten egg. (For those who want to ring the change he explains how to substitute cottage cheese. I recommend this version and guarantee that it will delight your guests and confound anyone who hasn't read this book.)

Having done food promotions all over the world, Anton Edelmann has had the opportunity to see the preparation of authentic and traditional dishes in every part of the globe. He has used a number of fresh and colourful Asian recipes here while also including such robust winter dishes as the superb braised knuckle of veal which I learned to call Kalbshaxen, a slow-roasted duck and that lovely example of French provincial cuisine, the navarin of lamb.

This user-friendly book has been lovingly created for amateurs and not for professional chefs. The processes are simple; the results impressive. But I warn you, Anton, these dishes are soon going to be appearing on restaurant menus everywhere. And if I often cook these dishes and bask in the glory of them, don't expect me always to admit where the recipes came from.

Len Deighton

INTRODUCTION

The inspiration for this book has come from my many years of working for The Savoy, and the reactions we have had from our guests. The hotel is seen as the bastion of tradition. Yet while it certainly keeps the best of the old, its lasting success has been because it has always been ahead of the times and a trend-setter.

■

It is my opinion that chefs have been guilty in the past of making recipes too complicated and expensive for people to cook easily at home. At The Savoy we are always able to buy the rarest and best ingredients at almost any time of year. We also have over a hundred highly trained chefs working day and night. But of course I realize that very few people have our supplies or trained chefs at their disposal, so in writing this book I have attempted to present a selection of recipes which the cook at home can prepare successfully.

Some of the recipes are simple, others are more complicated; some are easily affordable, others are 'treats'. But all have clear instructions to take you through each stage of the preparation, with lots of tips that I hope will help. All of the recipes have been thoroughly tested, so I feel confident that if you follow them carefully, you will have success. Then, you can go on to develop your own interpretation of the dish. After all, recipes in a book should inspire the cook; the pictures should stimulate the imagination. I hope to pass on to you some of my knowledge and techniques, so that you can feel confident to experiment. Even for me the learning never finishes....

Home cooks today know more about food than they ever did before, and have more confidence. They are embracing the new influences of foreign cuisines, from all over Europe, America and, most recently, Asia, while still retaining the traditional. The result is a simple, bold and unfussy cuisine that is truly exciting.

■

To create good food, it is essential to have good ingredients. Always buy the best you can afford. And seek the guidance of the experts, particularly when buying meat: it is important to go to a good butcher and to use his expertize to help you choose the right cut of meat for a recipe.

■

A colleague of mine once said, 'If you are serious about good cooking, a good stock is essential'. This is a sentiment with which I entirely agree. The stocks, or essences, and most of the sauces that are essential for the recipes in this book can be prepared in advance and refrigerated or frozen until they are needed. Once these are prepared, it leaves the cook free to get on with the transformation of the raw ingredients into a finished dish, a process which is fascinating, and the result a delight for the cook.

■

To my mind, a kitchen without herbs is like a language without grammar. Herbs enhance and bring out the flavour and characteristics of the food to which they are added, and some dishes are unthinkable without a specific herb. It is hard to imagine marinated salmon without dill, a juicy tomato salad without basil, or roast lamb without rosemary.

Apart from adding wonderful flavour and colour, herbs are also good for the health, stimulating digestion and enabling the cook to use less salt for seasoning.

Wherever possible, use fresh herbs, and pick the leaves from the stalks and snip or chop at the last moment, so that none of the natural oils are lost. Never overheat herbs or burn them in butter or oil. If you are frying whole leaves, do this very briefly so they retain their bright colour.

■

All five senses should be awakened and stimulated by the preparation and the eating of food. From the careful selection of ingredients, through the appropriate cooking techniques, to the precise amount of seasoning needed to intensify the flavour of the dish, all the senses are employed.

It is the sight, sound, touch, aroma and taste involved that transforms cooking and eating from a necessity to a delight.

May I wish you the best of luck. And bon appétit!

Anton Edelmann

NOTES TO THE COOK

Instructions for basic preparations such as peeling tomatoes, toasting nuts, and so on are given in boxes. Where these preparations are required in a subsequent individual recipe, a page reference denotes that detailed instructions can be found elsewhere in the book.

A NOTE FOR AMERICAN COOKS: Where the name of an ingredient or a term is different in the US, the equivalent is given in square brackets.

MEASUREMENTS: Both metric and imperial measures are given. These are not exact equivalents, so use one set of measures only when preparing a recipe as they are not interchangeable. In addition, American cup and spoon measures have been given where required (they appear as the third measure for each ingredient).

SPOON MEASURES: Metric spoon measures were used for testing (1 tbsp = 15ml, 1 tsp = 5 ml); these are near exact equivalents for American standard spoon measures. All are measured level unless otherwise stated.

EGGS: All eggs used for testing were size 3 [US extra large], unless otherwise specified in an individual recipe.

FLOUR: All flour used for testing was plain flour [US all-purpose flour], unless otherwise specified in an individual recipe.

SUGAR: All sugar used for testing was granulated sugar, unless otherwise specified in an individual recipe.

THE BUILDING
BLOCKS

HERE we deal with the essentials – the basic essences (stocks), sauces, dressings, pastries and so on. These can be compared with the foundations you lay down when building a house. Once these are prepared, you can build your dish on them.

It is important that the cook gives time and care to these fundamental preparations. However, I do not expect you to spend hours and much money on turning ten pounds of veal bones into a veal gravy, or large quantities of sole or turbot bones into the best fish essence. Instead, I suggest here a small but very versatile selection of essences, sauces and dressings.

Chicken concentrate is the one basic sauce in this book. It is the foundation on which we build all the other meat sauces. By adding roasted, grilled or poached trimmings or bones, or infusions of herbs and vegetables, or different types of alcohol, we introduce new flavours and develop an individual sauce for each dish.

The recipes here are simple and good fun to make, but the results are of a very high and professional standard.

VEGETABLE ESSENCE

Makes about 1 litre / 1³/4 pints / 1 US quart

Use this aromatic essence for poaching fish and poultry, cooking vegetables, or in sauces and soups.

1 small fennel bulb
2 celery stalks
2 onions
2 carrots, weighing about 200 g / 7 oz
225 g / 8 oz celeriac [US celery root] or
    additional celery
2 leeks, white and pale green parts only
1 large garlic clove

2 tbsp vegetable oil
2 star anise
1/4 tsp black peppercorns
1/2 tsp coriander seeds
1 small bay leaf
salt
juice of 1/2 lime
200 ml / 7 fl oz / 7/8 cup dry white wine

Trim and finely chop the fennel and celery. Peel and finely chop the onions, carrots and celeriac. Trim the leeks, cut lengthwise in half and wash well, then slice finely. Peel and slice the garlic.

Heat the oil in a large saucepan or stockpot over low heat and cook the onions until soft and translucent, stirring often. Add the remaining prepared vegetables and 150 ml / 1/4 pint / 2/3 cup water. Mix well, then cover and cook gently for about 30 minutes, stirring occasionally. If necessary, add a little more water to prevent the vegetables sticking.

Meanwhile, coarsely crush the star anise, peppercorns and coriander seeds with the base of a heavy pan.

Add the crushed spices to the vegetables together with the bay leaf and a little salt. Pour in 1.35 litres / 2¹/4 pints / 5¹/3 cups water and bring to the boil. Simmer for about 20 minutes.

Stir in the lime juice and wine. Remove the pan from the heat, cover and set aside in a cool place to infuse for 12 hours.

Strain the essence through a fine sieve. It can be kept in the refrigerator for a day, or frozen.

MUSSEL ESSENCE

Makes at least 600 ml / 1 pint / 2¹/₂ cups

The yield for this essence recipe will vary according to how much liquor is in the mussel shells. Use the essence for soups and fish sauces or for poaching fish.

T I P

Freeze this essence in convenient quantities.

700 g / 1¹/₂ lb small fresh mussels
1 onion
1 leek, white and pale green parts only
1 celery stalk
2 garlic cloves

2 sprigs of fresh lemon thyme
300 ml / ¹/₂ pint / 1¹/₄ cups dry white wine
300 ml / ¹/₂ pint / 1¹/₄ cups Chicken Essence
 (see page 14)

Scrub the mussels well under cold running water, and scrape off the beards and any barnacles. All the shells should be tightly closed, or should close if tapped sharply on the work surface; discard any mussels that remain open or that have cracked or broken shells.

Peel and finely chop the onion. Trim the leek, cut it lengthwise in half and wash well, then slice finely. Trim and finely slice the celery. Peel the garlic and chop to a paste (see box below).

Combine the mussels, prepared vegetables, garlic, thyme, wine and chicken essence in a large saucepan. Cover and cook over a high heat for 3–5 minutes or until the mussel shells are all open. Shake the pan frequently.

Drain the mussels in a colander set in a large, deep bowl. Discard any mussels that have remained stubbornly closed, then tip the remainder into another bowl. Cover with a kitchen cloth and leave until cool enough to handle.

Remove the mussels from their shells, working over the bowl containing the mussel essence so that all the liquor from the shells is retained. Set the mussels aside.

Ladle the essence into another bowl, leaving any sand or sediment at the bottom.

TO CHOP GARLIC TO A PASTE

Set the flat side of a large knife on top of the garlic clove and strike the knife with the side of your fist. Peel off the garlic skin. Chop the garlic roughly, then sprinkle it with a little salt and leave for 1 minute. Finely chop and crush the garlic to a paste.

CHICKEN ESSENCE

Makes about 2.5 litres / 4 pints / 2¹/2 US quarts

This basic essence should be strong in flavour. If it is weak, boil it to reduce after it has been strained. To achieve a clear essence, skim it frequently.

2 chickens, each weighing about 1.2 kg / 2³/4 lb
2 onions
2 carrots
2 celery stalks
1 tsp black peppercorns

1 bay leaf
2 sprigs of fresh thyme
a few parsley stalks [US parsley stems]
salt

Cut off the chicken breasts and reserve them for another dish. Pull off as much of the skin from the chickens as possible and discard it. Chop the chicken carcasses, wings and leg portions into pieces and put them in a stockpot or large saucepan. Cover with 3.75 litres / 6 pints / 3³/4 quarts cold water and bring slowly to simmering point, skimming often to remove all the froth that rises. Simmer for 10 minutes.

Peel or trim the vegetables and chop them coarsely. Crush the peppercorns coarsely with the base of a small heavy pan.

Add the vegetables, herbs, peppercorns and a little salt to the pan. Continue simmering very gently for 1 hour.

Turn up the heat a little so the liquid is simmering a little more quickly, but not boiling. Simmer for a further 1 hour.

Strain the essence and allow to cool completely. Remove any fat from the surface before using.

TIPS

Add only a little salt because the flavour will be intensified in the reduced liquid. It is better to add more seasoning to the dish in which you use the essence.

Fresh herbs are always best, but if fresh thyme is not available, you can use 1 tsp dried thyme.

A boiling fowl [US stewing chicken] will give excellent flavour to the essence. You can also make the essence using carcasses and bones left from raw or cooked birds. Collect them in freezer bags and store in the freezer until you have 4–6, then make the essence.

Freeze the essence in convenient quantities.

RIGHT
The Savoy's Chicken Pie with Chicken Essence (see page 110)

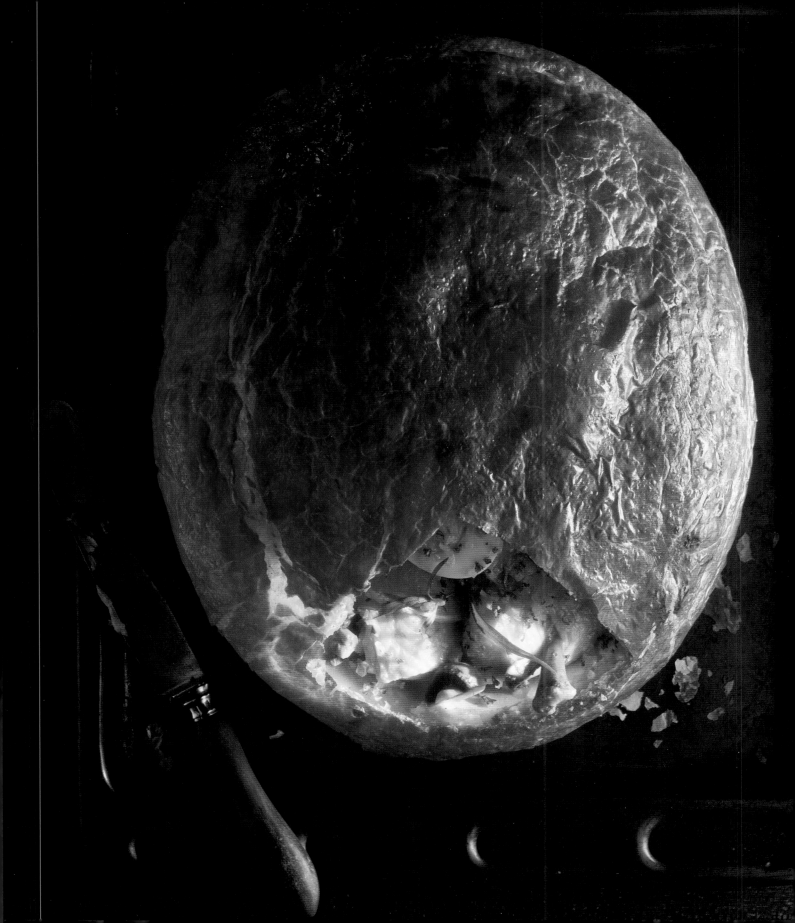

CHICKEN CONCENTRATE

Makes about 700 ml / scant 1¹/4 pints / nearly 3 cups

This is my basic sauce, for meat, poultry and vegetables – even fish – devised specially for the home cook, to give a result very similar to a sauce made in a professional kitchen. The flavour of the sauce is sweet and intense, and it is ideal for taking on other flavours from herbs and aromatics, making it wonderfully versatile.

400 g / 14 oz chicken carcasses and bones
3 tbsp vegetable oil
2 onions
2 carrots
1 leek
1 celery stalk
2 tomatoes

80 g / 2³/4 oz / 5 tbsp tomato paste
2 garlic cloves
1 small bay leaf
1 sprig of fresh thyme
250 ml / 8 fl oz / 1 cup dry white wine
2.5 litres / 4 pints / 2¹/2 quarts Chicken Essence (see page 14)

Preheat the oven to 220°C / 425°F / gas 7.

Chop the chicken carcasses and bones into pieces as small as possible. Heat a roasting pan on top of the stove. Add the oil and chicken bones. Transfer to the oven and roast for 10 minutes. Meanwhile, peel or trim and coarsely chop all the vegetables. Add the vegetables to the chicken bones and continue roasting for 10 minutes or until the bones are browned.

Coarsely chop the tomatoes and add to the pan with the tomato paste, peeled garlic cloves and herbs. Stir well and roast for 10 minutes longer.

Pour the mixture into a stockpot or other large pan, scraping the roasting pan well. Add the wine to the roasting pan and bring to the boil on top of the stove, stirring to dissolve the browned bits on the bottom of the pan. Pour the wine into the stockpot and stir to mix. Bring back to the boil.

Add the chicken essence, bring to the boil again and simmer until reduced by half, skimming from time to time.

Strain through muslin [US cheesecloth] or a fine sieve. This is now our basic sauce and can be frozen in small quantities.

TIPS

The finer the bones are chopped, the more flavour they will release.

The colour of this sauce depends on the browning of the bones and tomato paste. You can vary the colour according to how long you roast the ingredients. However, be careful not to burn them because this will make the sauce bitter.

SUN-DRIED TOMATO SAUCE

Makes about 300 ml / 1/2 pint / 1 1/4 cups

Dried tomatoes have a wonderfully intense flavour, particularly if they have been dried in the sun. Tomatoes are easy to dry at home, and can be kept in the refrigerator for several weeks, ready to use in sauces such as this or in many other dishes.

1/2 onion
1 garlic clove
1 tbsp olive oil
150 g / 5 oz sun-dried tomatoes packed in oil
1 tbsp tomato paste
1 sprig of fresh thyme

2 tsp fresh oregano leaves
350 ml / 12 fl oz / 1 1/2 cups Chicken Essence (see page 14)
cayenne pepper
salt and freshly ground black pepper
2 tsp fresh marjoram leaves

Peel and chop the onion. Peel the garlic and chop to a paste (see page 13). Heat the oil in a saucepan over low heat and cook the onion until soft and translucent, stirring often. Add the garlic and cook gently for 1 minute longer.

Drain and dry the sun-dried tomatoes. Add to the pan with the tomato paste, thyme and oregano. Cook gently for 2 minutes, stirring frequently.

Add the chicken essence. Bring to the boil and simmer for 10 minutes. Discard the thyme sprig.

Purée the sauce in a blender or food processor, then press it through a fine sieve into a clean saucepan. Season with a little cayenne and pepper, and salt if necessary.

Chop the marjoram finely and stir into the sauce, then reheat for serving.

TO DRY TOMATOES

Peel each tomato (see page 74), then cut it lengthwise into quarters. Scrape out and discard all the seeds. Spread out the tomato quarters on a rack and sprinkle them lightly with salt. Leave to dry in a warm place or in a very low oven for about 12 hours. When dried, the tomatoes will be slightly shrivelled (the salt draws out the moisture which will evaporate in the heat) and a deeper red in colour. Put them in a jar and fill the jar with olive oil. The tomatoes will keep in the refrigerator for several weeks.

WHITE WINE SAUCE

Makes 300 ml / ¹/2 pint / 1¹/4 cups

This is a very versatile sauce, particularly good with poached fish. If you mix it half and half with chicken concentrate (see recipe on page 16), you can also use it for poultry and meat dishes.

1 onion
¹/2 large carrot
1 garlic clove
250 ml / 8 fl oz / 1 cup dry white wine
100 ml / 3¹/2 fl oz / 7 tbsp white wine vinegar
1 tsp black peppercorns

¹/2 tsp juniper berries
¹/2 tsp coriander seeds
500 ml / 16 fl oz / 2 cups double cream
  [US heavy whipping cream]
45 g / 1¹/2 oz / 3 tbsp unsalted butter
salt and freshly ground black pepper

Peel and roughly chop the onion, carrot and garlic. Combine with 500 ml / 16 fl oz / 2 cups water, the wine and vinegar in a bowl. Coarsely crush the peppercorns, juniper berries and coriander seeds with the base of a heavy pan and add to the bowl. Leave to marinate for 1¹/2 – 2 hours.

Strain the mixture through a fine sieve into a saucepan, pressing down on the vegetables and spices to extract the maximum liquid and flavour. Bring to the boil and boil to reduce to about 170 ml / 6 fl oz / ³/4 cup.

Stir in the cream and boil until slightly thickened.

Add the butter and stir until it has melted into the sauce. Season with salt and pepper, and serve.

TIP
After reducing the marinated mixture, it can be cooled and refrigerated overnight. Then add the cream and finish the sauce as explained left.

WHITE BATTER

Makes 300 ml / ¹/2 pint / 1¹/4 cups

This is the basic batter used for coating small pieces of meat and poultry, fish and vegetables before frying.

150 g / 5 oz / 1 cup strong plain flour
  [US all-purpose flour]
salt and freshly ground black pepper

2 tbsp white wine vinegar
1 egg, size 2 [US extra large]

Sift the flour into a bowl and make a well in the centre. Add some salt and pepper. Pour 175 ml / 6 fl oz / ³/4 cup very cold water, the vinegar and beaten egg into the well. Whisk the liquids together, then gradually whisk in the flour from the sides to make a smooth batter. Strain the batter through a fine sieve before using.

BUTTER SAUCE

Makes 200 ml / 7 fl oz / 7/8 cup

This unctuous sauce can be served with meat, poultry, fish or vegetable dishes.

3 shallots
150 g / 5 oz / 10 tbsp unsalted butter
about 100 ml / 3 1/2 fl oz / 7 tbsp Chicken Essence (see page 14)
100 ml / 3 1/2 fl oz / 7 tbsp dry white wine, preferably from Provence

1/4 tsp white peppercorns
1 star anise
salt
cayenne pepper

TIPS
Butter sauce should be served as soon as possible after it is made, and not allowed to cool. If you try to reheat it, it will separate.

If serving with fish, the flavour of the sauce will be better if you replace half of the chicken essence with mussel essence (see recipe on page 13).

Should the sauce separate, whisk it into a little reduced double cream [US heavy whipping cream].

Peel and finely chop the shallots. Melt 15 g / 1/2 oz / 1 tbsp of the butter in a heavy-based saucepan over low heat and cook the shallots until soft and nearly translucent, stirring often.

Stir in the chicken essence and wine. Crush the peppercorns and star anise with the base of a small heavy pan and add to the saucepan. Bring to the boil and boil until the liquid is reduced by three-quarters.

Remove from the heat and leave to cool for 2 minutes. Cut the remaining butter into small cubes. Return the sauce to a very low heat and gradually whisk in the rest of the butter, a few pieces at a time. If the sauce becomes too thick, add a little more chicken essence.

Strain the sauce through a fine sieve into a clean saucepan, pressing down on the shallots and seasonings in the sieve to extract maximum liquid and flavour. Season with salt and cayenne. If necessary, set the pan in a larger pan of simmering water to keep it warm until serving; do not allow the sauce to boil.

SPICY VEGETABLE SAUCE

Makes 400 ml / 14 fl oz / 1 3/4 cups

This sweet and spicy sauce is excellent with fish, poultry, pasta and vegetable dishes. It is based on equal prepared weights of onion, sweet pepper and apple.

1 onion
1 red sweet pepper
25 g / 3/4 oz / 1 1/2 tbsp unsalted butter
1 1/2 tbsp vegetable oil
1 small apple
1/2 tsp curry powder
a pinch of saffron (optional)

350 ml / 12 fl oz / 1 1/2 cups Chicken Essence (see page 14) or Vegetable Essence (see page 12)
salt and freshly ground black pepper
3 tbsp double cream [US heavy whipping cream] or crème fraîche

Peel and finely chop the onion. Remove the core and seeds from the red pepper, then finely chop the flesh.

Heat the butter and oil in a saucepan over low heat and cook the onion until soft and translucent, stirring often. Stir in the red pepper, then cover and cook gently for 10 minutes.

Peel, core and slice the apple. Add to the pan with the curry powder and saffron and stir well. Cook, covered, for a further 5 minutes.

Add 300 ml / 1/2 pint / 1 1/4 cups of the chicken and vegetable essence and bring to the boil. Simmer, covered, for 20 minutes.

Purée the sauce in a blender or food processor, then pass it through a fine sieve into a clean saucepan, pressing down on the vegetables in the sieve to extract maximum liquid and flavour. Stir in the remaining essence, and season with salt and pepper.

Reheat and stir in the cream before serving.

SHERRY VINAIGRETTE

Makes 150 ml / ¹/4 pint / ²/3 cup

This simple vinaigrette can be applied to many dishes.

120 ml / 4 fl oz / ¹/2 cup olive oil
2 tbsp sherry vinegar

salt and freshly ground black pepper

Whisk the oil and vinegar together in a bowl. Season to taste with salt and pepper.

Variation
PLUM TOMATO AND HERB VINAIGRETTE: Peel 200 g / 7 oz ripe but firm plum tomatoes and remove the seeds (see page 74). Cut the tomato flesh neatly into very small dice. Just before using, stir the tomato dice into the sherry vinaigrette, with 4 tbsp chopped mixed fresh herbs such as chives, parsley, basil and dill. Taste and adjust the seasoning.

For some recipes, the dressing is used warm: Heat the sherry vinaigrette in a saucepan until it is lukewarm, stirring constantly; do not allow it to boil. Stir in the tomato dice and herbs just before serving.

SOY VINAIGRETTE

Makes 100 ml / 3¹/2 fl oz / 7 tbsp

TIP

If more convenient, you can substitute 1 tbsp orange juice concentrate for the orange juice reduction.

100 ml / 3¹/2 fl oz / 7 tbsp orange juice
1 tbsp white wine vinegar
1 tbsp soy sauce

4 tbsp olive oil
freshly ground black pepper

Put the orange juice in a small pan and boil until reduced to 1 tbsp. Set aside to cool completely.

Combine all the ingredients in a bowl and whisk well to mix.

Variation
SOY AND BALSAMIC VINAIGRETTE: Substitute 1¹/2 tbsp balsamic vinegar for the white wine vinegar, and groundnut oil [US peanut oil] for the olive oil.

CURRY DRESSING

Makes 200 ml / 7 fl oz / 7/8 cup

This dressing can be used for fish, shellfish or chicken, in dishes that include fruit such as apples, pears or pineapple.

1 tsp white wine vinegar
1 egg yolk
3 tbsp extra virgin olive oil
135 ml / 4 1/2 fl oz / 9 tbsp sunflower oil
1 tsp lemon juice
salt and freshly ground black pepper

For the curry mixture
3 tbsp finely chopped shallot
3 tbsp finely chopped carrot
3 tbsp finely chopped celery
1 tsp lemon juice
100 ml / 3 1/2 fl oz / 7 tbsp dry white wine
2 tsp chopped mixed fresh dill and chives
1/2 tsp ground coriander
1 tbsp curry powder

First make the curry mixture. Combine all the ingredients in a saucepan. Bring to the boil, stirring frequently, then simmer very gently until reduced by two-thirds. Strain the mixture into a bowl, pressing the vegetables in the sieve to extract the maximum liquid and flavour. Allow to cool.

Whisk the vinegar with the egg yolk. Whisk in the cold curry mixture. Slowly whisk in the oils, a few drops at first and then in a thin stream. Season with the lemon juice, salt and pepper.

TIP
If the dressing is too thick, whisk in a little water, a few drops at a time.

MAYONNAISE

Makes just over 500 ml / 16 fl oz / 2 cups

2 egg yolks
2 tbsp white wine vinegar
2 tsp Dijon mustard

a few drops of Worcestershire sauce
salt and freshly ground white pepper
500 ml / 16 fl oz / 2 cups vegetable oil

Combine the egg yolks, vinegar, mustard and Worcestershire sauce in a food processor. Season with salt and pepper. Mix together until smoothly blended. With the machine running, add the oil slowly through the feed tube. Start with a few drops of oil, then increase to a thin stream.

When all the oil has been incorporated and the mayonnaise is thick, taste it and add more mustard, vinegar, salt and pepper if required.

RIGHT
Salad of Lobster in a Curry Dressing (see page 84)

PESTO SAUCE

Makes about 350 ml / 12 fl oz / 1 1/2 cups

This is one of the most useful sauces to have on hand in your kitchen because it can be used in so many different dishes, be they meat, fish or pasta. It enhances flavours and character without being overpowering.

15 g / 1/2 oz / 1 tbsp shelled pistachio nuts
60 g / 2 oz Parmesan cheese
60 g / 2 oz / 1 cup fresh basil leaves
30 g / 1 oz / 1/2 cup fresh parsley sprigs
2 garlic cloves

30 g / 1 oz / 1/4 cup pine nuts
15 g / 1/2 oz / 1 1/2 tbsp walnut pieces
250 ml / 8 fl oz / 1 cup olive oil
salt and freshly ground black pepper

Skin the pistachio nuts (see box). Finely grate the Parmesan. Wash and dry the basil and parsley. Peel and coarsely chop the garlic.

Put the basil, parsley, pine nuts, walnuts, pistachios, Parmesan and garlic in a food processor. Add half the oil. Work until the ingredients are finely chopped.

Gradually add the remaining oil through the feed tube, with the motor running. Season to taste. Process again briefly.

TO SKIN PISTACHIO NUTS
Put the shelled nuts in a saucepan of milk, bring to the boil and drain. Rub the nuts in a coarse towel to remove the skins.

TIP

It's worth making pesto in large amounts because it keeps well in a tightly covered jar in the refrigerator.

RED PEPPER PESTO

Makes 450 ml / 3/4 pint / just under 2 cups

Red pepper pesto can be used to coat all kinds of grilled fish. It also goes well with charcoal-grilled chicken.

3 red sweet peppers
3 garlic cloves
1/2 fresh hot red chilli pepper
30 g / 1 oz Parmesan cheese

60 g / 2 oz / 1/2 cup slivered almonds
1/2 tsp white wine vinegar
125 ml / 4 fl oz / 1/2 cup olive oil
salt and freshly ground black pepper

Peel the sweet peppers using a swivel-bladed vegetable peeler. Cut each pepper lengthwise into quarters and remove the core, seeds and white ribs. Peel the garlic cloves and chop to a paste (see page 13). Remove the seeds and core from the chilli pepper. Grate the Parmesan.

Put the red pepper quarters and chilli pepper in a food processor and blend until smooth. Add the garlic, Parmesan, slivered almonds and white wine vinegar and blend briefly to mix. Gradually add the olive oil to make a paste. Season with salt and pepper.

TIPS

Chill the pesto for about 1 1/2 hours before using.

For extra bite add 2-3 drops of Tabasco sauce.

VANILLA CUSTARD SAUCE

Makes about 500 ml / 16 fl oz / 2 cups

400 ml / 14 fl oz / 1³/4 cups milk
1 vanilla pod [US vanilla bean]
7 egg yolks

80 g / generous 2¹/2 oz / 6¹/2 tbsp caster sugar [US granulated sugar]

Put the milk in a heavy-based saucepan. Split the vanilla pod open and add to the pan. Heat until bubbles form around the edge. Remove from the heat and set aside in a warm place to infuse for 10 minutes.

Meanwhile, whisk the egg yolks with the sugar in a bowl set over a pan of hot water until the sugar has dissolved and the mixture is pale, thick and increased in volume. Incorporate half of the warm milk, whisking well.

Heat the milk remaining in the pan to just below a simmer. Gradually add the milk and egg yolk mixture in a steady stream, stirring constantly with a wooden spoon. Cook over low heat, stirring, until the sauce thickens enough to coat the back of the spoon thinly.

Strain the sauce through a fine sieve into a bowl. Set the bowl in a container of iced water to prevent the sauce from cooking further. Leave to cool.

Variation
MINT CUSTARD SAUCE: After straining the sauce, stir in 2 tbsp very finely chopped fresh mint.

PASTA DOUGH

Makes about 450 g / 1 lb

250 g / 9 oz / 2¼ cups flour
¼ tsp salt
2 whole eggs

5 egg yolks
1 tbsp olive oil

Sift the flour. Combine all the ingredients in a food processor and process to a well mixed dough. Turn the dough on to a well floured surface and knead for 5–10 minutes or until the dough is quite smooth and elastic.

Shape the dough into a ball, cover and set aside in a cool place to rest for 1 hour.

Cut the dough into pieces about the size of a lemon. Work with one piece at a time, keeping the remaining dough covered. Set the pasta machine so the rollers are widest apart. Feed the piece of dough through over and over, folding the sheet of dough each time, until it is smooth and elastic.

To roll out the dough, set the machine to the next narrowest setting and feed the dough through. Set the machine down another notch, and feed the dough through again, without folding it. Continue until you reach the setting specified in the recipe.

If the pasta dough is to be used for lasagne or filled shapes such as tortellini, cut it as soon as it is rolled out. If it is to be used for tagliatelle or other noodles, leave it to dry for about 20 minutes before cutting.

SWEET PASTRY

Makes 675 g / 1½ lb

225 g / 8 oz / 2 sticks unsalted butter, at
*   room temperature*
100 g / 3½ oz / ½ cup caster sugar
*   [US granulated sugar]*

1 egg
350 g / 12 oz / 2⅓ cups flour
a pinch of salt

Using a wooden spoon, cream the butter with the sugar until the mixture is smooth and very pale. Lightly beat the egg, then gradually mix it into the creamed mixture.

Add the flour and salt, a little at a time, and slowly stir into the creamed mixture. When the mixture becomes too stiff to stir, continue mixing in the flour with your hands. Bring the mixture together into a smooth ball.

Wrap the dough and leave it to rest in the refrigerator for at least 1 hour before using.

PUFF PASTRY

Makes 700 g / 1¹/2 lb

TIPS

The butter should not be straight from the refrigerator, nor should it be softened to room temperature. If it were taken from a cool larder, it would have the perfect consistency.

Puff pastry consists of many horizontal layers of pastry dough. To ensure that it rises evenly, the layers must all be parallel. So after cutting a shape, tap all around the sides with a knife to be sure the top surface is completely level and the sides are straight.

I know that puff pastry is very labour intensive but although the quality of commercial frozen puff pastry is good, it could never be as good as your own. The recipe here uses butter, which gives the pastry an incomparable flavour.

350 g / 12 oz / 3 sticks unsalted butter
350 g / 12 oz / 2¹/2 cups flour
¹/2 tsp salt

9 tbsp iced water
a squeeze of lemon juice

Put 250 g / 9 oz / 2 sticks + 1 tbsp of the butter on a cool surface with 90 g / 3 oz / ¹/2 cup + 2 tbsp of the flour. Work the butter and flour together with your fingertips until they are well mixed. Form into a square block that is about 4 cm / 1¹/2 inches thick. Wrap and refrigerate until firm but not hard.

Put the remaining flour on the cool surface and add the salt and the remaining butter. Rub together until the mixture resembles fine breadcrumbs. Add the iced water and lemon juice and mix together to make a smooth, elastic dough. Shape the dough into a ball.

Lightly flour the surface. Cut a cross in the top of the ball, to one-third of its depth. Open out the points of the cross, then roll out the dough to make a

4-pointed star that is 5 mm / ¹/4 inch thick.

Place the butter and flour block in the centre of the dough and fold the points or flaps over, working anti-clockwise. Press the edges to seal them well.

Roll out the dough into an oblong about 5 mm / ¹/4 inch thick. Fold over the two short sides to meet in the middle, then fold the dough in half to make four equal layers. This is called a double-turn. Cover the dough with a damp cloth and leave in the refrigerator for at least 30 minutes.

Roll out the dough into an oblong again, then fold it as before and rest in the refrigerator. Repeat the rolling and folding three more times, then leave the dough, covered, in the refrigerator to rest for several hours, or preferably overnight, before using.

TO MAKE PASTRY DISCS

Roll out 7 oz Puff Pastry (see above) to about 3-mm / ¹/8-inch thickness. With a 7-cm / 2³/4-inch round cutter, cut out 8 discs. Place the discs on a baking sheet and prick with a fork. Beat 1 egg yolk with 1 tsp water and brush over discs. Chill for 5 minutes to allow the egg to dry, then brush the discs again. Sprinkle 4 with ¹/4 tsp poppy seeds and 4 with ¹/4 tsp sesame seeds. Chill for 1 hour. Heat the oven to 200°C / 400°F / gas 6. Bake the discs for 10 minutes or until golden brown. Then cool on a wire rack.

SPONGE CAKE

Makes a 16- to 17-cm / 6¹/2- to 7-inch cake

This cake is delicious served plain to accompany tea or coffee, or it can be dressed up with a sprinkling of sugar or whipped cream and served with a sorbet or ice cream or with raspberry sauce (see recipe on page 170).

15 g / ¹/2 oz / 1 tbsp unsalted butter
150 ml / ¹/4 pint / ²/3 cup eggs (about 4 eggs)

120 g / 4 oz / 10 tbsp caster sugar
* [US superfine sugar]*
120 g / 4 oz / 1 cup flour [US cake flour]

Heat the oven to 180°C / 350°F / gas 4. Butter a deep 16–17 cm / 6¹/2–7 inch round cake pan and line the bottom with a disc of greaseproof paper [US wax paper].

Melt the butter in a small pan, then remove from the heat and set aside.

Put the eggs and sugar in a large heat-proof bowl and set over a pan of simmering water. Whisk until the mixture is pale and very thick and much increased in volume. When the whisk is lifted, the mixture should drop back in a ribbon trail on itself.

Remove the bowl from the pan of water. Sift the flour over the surface of the mixture, a little at a time, and fold it in along with the melted butter.

Transfer the mixture to the prepared pan. Bake for 35–45 minutes or until the cake is risen and firm to the touch. A skewer inserted into the centre should come out clean. Turn out on to a wire rack and leave to cool.

TIPS

If the cake is browning too quickly towards the end of the baking, cover the top with foil.

If you intend to use the sponge within 12 hours of baking, omit the butter. The cake will be lighter and, of course, healthier.

28

SOUPS

AFTER meat roasted on a spit, soup was probably the first thing people ever cooked. And for good reason: soup can be thick and warming in winter, fruity and refreshing in summer, and it is nourishing, with health properties far beyond its modest status. Soup can make a delightful meal on its own, eaten with crusty bread, or be a first course, in harmony with the rest of the meal. Yet, despite these remarkable attributes, soup has often been regarded as a 'second division' player.

Making soup can be very exciting, and it can engage your imagination endlessly. There are many different kinds of broth soups such as consommé, which can be garnished with ravioli, wontons, shellfish and vegetables. There are those soups thickened with vegetables like potatoes or with rice or barley, or with flour, which is less popular these days.

The base of all soups is a good strong essence. With that foundation, almost everything edible can be used in the making of a soup, from snails to shark's fin: all kinds of meat, fresh or smoked, poultry and game, vegetables, herbs and spices, barley, rice, cheese, fruits – the list is endless. Too many people make soups with leftovers; they do not see the intriguing possibilities of other, fresh ingredients.

A good soup can have flavours that are as complex and exciting as anything else in cooking. Soup deserves more recognition, from the cook and gourmet alike.

CHICKEN BROTH WITH RICOTTA RAVIOLI

Serves 4

The essence for this broth should be clear and strong, so if possible make it with a boiling fowl and skim it frequently and thoroughly while it is simmering. It is boiled to reduce the quantity by half, to concentrate the flavour.

2 litres / 3¹/₂ pints / 2 US quarts Chicken
  Essence (see page 14)
1 very small skinned and boned chicken breast
  [US chicken breast half]
salt and freshly ground black pepper
15 g / ¹/₂ oz / 1 tbsp unsalted butter
25 g / ³/₄ oz Parmesan cheese

75 g / 2¹/₂ oz / ¹/₃ cup ricotta cheese
1 whole egg
grated zest of ¹/₂ unwaxed lemon
freshly grated nutmeg
¹/₃ quantity Pasta Dough (see page 26)
1 egg yolk
1 tbsp chopped fresh chives

Heat the oven to 180°C / 350°F / gas 4.

Put the chicken essence in a wide saucepan, bring to the boil and boil until reduced by half.

Meanwhile, season the chicken breast with salt and pepper. Melt the butter in a small flameproof casserole over moderate heat. Add the chicken breast and turn to coat with the butter. Cover and transfer to the oven. Cook for 10 minutes or until the chicken is opaque and just firm. Remove from the oven and leave to cool.

Very finely chop the chicken in a food processor. Or you can use the fine blade/disc in a mincer [US meat grinder].

Grate the Parmesan finely and add to the food processor. Add the ricotta, whole egg and lemon zest. Season with nutmeg, salt and pepper. Process again briefly to blend all the ingredients together evenly.

Using a pasta machine on the second narrowest setting, roll out the pasta dough. With a 6-cm / 2¹/₂-inch round cutter, cut out 12 discs.

Lightly beat the egg yolk with ¹/₂ tsp water. Brush this egg wash around the edge of each disc of pasta dough and spoon the chicken mixture into the centre. Fold the discs over to make half-moon shapes, pressing the edges well to seal.

Bring the reduced chicken essence back to the boil. Turn down the heat so the liquid is just simmering, then add the ravioli and poach them for about 4 minutes.

With a slotted spoon, transfer the ravioli to warmed soup plates. Taste the broth and adjust the seasoning if necessary, then ladle it over the ravioli. Sprinkle with the chives and serve.

VEGETABLE AND HERB BROTH

Serves 4

1 red onion
1 leek, white and pale green parts only
2 small carrots
1/2 head of Chinese leaves [US Napa cabbage]
100 g / 3 1/2 oz potatoes
3 ripe but firm plum tomatoes
15 g / 1/2 oz / 1 tbsp unsalted butter
1 tbsp olive oil

1 litre / 1 3/4 pints / 1 quart Vegetable Essence (see page 12)
2 tbsp chopped mixed fresh herbs such as basil, flat-leaf (Italian) parsley and chervil
salt and freshly ground black pepper
8–12 French Bread Croûtes (see box)
4 tbsp freshly grated hard cheese, such as Sprinz, Parmesan or aged pecorino

Peel and chop the onion. Trim the leek, cut it lengthwise in half and wash well, then cut across into 5-mm / 1/4-inch pieces. Peel the carrots and cut across into 5-mm / 1/4-inch slices. Wash the Chinese leaves and drain them, then stack and cut across into fine strips. Peel the potatoes, cut into 5-mm / 1/4-inch dice and rinse well. Peel the tomatoes and remove the seeds (see page 74). Cut the flesh into 5-mm / 1/4-inch dice.

Heat the butter and oil in a large saucepan over a low heat and cook the onion until soft and translucent, stirring often. Add the leek and carrots, cover the pan and cook gently for 5 minutes, stirring occasionally.

Stir in the potatoes and vegetable essence and bring to the boil. Simmer, uncovered, for about 15 minutes. Add the Chinese leaves and continue simmering until all the vegetables are tender. Add the tomatoes and herbs to the soup, and season.

Put 2 or 3 croûtes in each bowl and ladle in the soup. Sprinkle the cheese on top and serve.

FRENCH BREAD CROÛTES

Heat the grill [US broiler]. Cut 1/2 small loaf of French bread (baguette) into very thin slices and spread them out on a baking sheet. Toast under the grill until golden brown on both sides.

COCK-A-LEEKIE WITH SCALLOPS

Serves 4

*225 g / 8 oz leeks, white and pale green
   parts only*
30 g / 1 oz / 2 tbsp unsalted butter
a pinch of sugar
salt and freshly ground black pepper
*1 litre / 1³/4 pints / 1 quart Chicken Essence
   (see page 14)*

225 g / 8 oz potatoes
4 large scallops [US sea scallops]
45 g / 1¹/2 oz / ¹/4 cup pitted prunes
2 tsp chopped fresh chives

TIP
If your prunes are not the no-need-to-soak variety, soak them in a little hot water first to plump them up.

Trim the leeks, cut them lengthwise in half and wash them well. Cut the leaves into 1-cm / ¹/2-inch squares.

Melt the butter in a saucepan over low heat and cook the leeks for 3–5 minutes or until soft, stirring often. Add the sugar and season with salt and pepper. Stir well, then add the chicken essence. Bring to the boil and simmer for 7 minutes.

Meanwhile, peel the potatoes and cut them into thin slices, then cut the slices into 1-cm / ¹/2-inch squares.

Remove any roe or coral from the scallops. Trim the hard, greyish-white gristly bit from each scallop, leaving just the tender white nut of meat. Cut each scallop into 1-cm / ¹/2-inch dice. Cut the prunes into small, neat pieces.

Add the potatoes to the soup and simmer for a further 3 minutes or until they are just tender.

Divide the scallops and prunes among 4 soup plates and ladle over the hot soup. Sprinkle with the chives and serve.

RIGHT
*Cock-a-Leekie with
Scallops*

VEGETABLE SOUP WITH BASIL AND GOAT'S CHEESE DUMPLINGS

Serves 4

1 large onion
1 garlic clove
2 young leeks, white and pale green parts only
1 red sweet pepper
2 ripe but firm plum tomatoes
60 g / 2 oz / ½ cup shelled fresh peas or
    frozen petit pois
15 g / ½ oz / 1 tbsp unsalted butter
2 tbsp olive oil
1 litre / 1¾ pints / 1 quart Chicken Essence
    (see page 14)

salt and freshly ground black pepper
chopped fresh basil, to garnish

For the dumplings
120 g / 4 oz soft goat's cheese
60 g / 2 oz / 1⅓ cups fine fresh white
    breadcrumbs
4 tsp chopped fresh basil
2 eggs

Peel and finely chop the onion. Peel the garlic and chop it to a paste (see page 13). Trim the leeks, cut them lengthwise in half and wash them well, then cut into 1-cm / ½-inch squares. Remove the core and seeds from the red pepper and cut the flesh into 1-cm / ½-inch squares. Peel the tomatoes and remove the seeds (see page 74). Cut the flesh neatly into 1-cm / ½-inch dice. Blanch the fresh peas in a small pan of boiling salted water for 5 minutes; drain. (If using frozen peas, just thaw them and drain well.)

Heat the butter and oil in a saucepan over a low heat and cook the onion until soft and translucent, stirring often. Add the garlic and cook gently another minute.

Stir in the leeks, cover the pan and cook gently until soft.

Add the red pepper and chicken essence.

Bring to the boil, then reduce the heat and simmer, uncovered, for about 8 minutes, skimming occasionally.

Meanwhile, make the dumplings. Put the goat's cheese in a bowl and mash it well with a fork. Add the breadcrumbs and basil and season with salt and pepper. Lightly beat the eggs and mix into the cheese mixture. With 2 teaspoons, shape the mixture into little egg-shaped dumplings (see box).

Add the dumplings to the soup and poach them gently for 3–4 minutes or until they are just firm and all the vegetables are tender. Just before the end of the cooking time, stir in the tomatoes and peas, being careful not to break up the dumplings.

Taste and adjust the seasoning. Sprinkle a little chopped basil on top and serve immediately.

TO SHAPE DUMPLINGS

Take a scoop of the mixture with one spoon, then use the other spoon to help mould an egg shape by turning and scooping the mixture from spoon to spoon. In French, these dumplings are called 'quenelles'.

SWEETCORN CHOWDER WITH SHELLFISH WONTONS

Serves 5

TIPS

Use fresh sweetcorn when it is in season. Pull off all the husks and silk, then cut the kernels from the cob with a knife.

You can use any shellfish for the wonton filling – langoustines, lobster meat, prawns or shrimp.

1 large onion
2 small leeks, white and pale green parts only
2 garlic cloves
30 g / 1 oz / 2 tbsp unsalted butter
2 tbsp vegetable oil
300 g / 10 oz / 1³/4 cups canned sweetcorn [US whole kernel corn]
1 litre / 1³/4 pints / 1 quart Chicken Essence (see page 14)
30 g / 1 oz Cheddar cheese
salt and freshly ground black pepper
a handful of baby spinach or sorrel

For the shellfish wontons
2 spring onions [US scallions]
¹/2 small, ripe but firm plum tomato
¹/2 avocado
30 g / 1 oz trimmed scallops
30 g / 1 oz peeled scampi (Dublin Bay prawns)
¹/2 tsp finely chopped fresh root ginger
cayenne pepper
10 wonton wrappers [US wonton skins], each about 7.5 cm/3 inches square
1 egg yolk
Chicken Essence (see page 14) or salted water

First make the wontons. Trim and finely chop the spring onions. Peel the tomato and remove the seeds (see page 74). Cut the flesh into fine dice. Peel the avocado and finely dice the flesh. Cut the scallop and scampi into small dice. Combine the prepared ingredients and ginger in a bowl and season with cayenne, salt and pepper.

Lay the wonton wrappers out flat. Divide the shellfish mixture among them, spooning it into the centre. Lightly beat the egg yolk with 1 tsp water and brush this egg wash around the edges of the wonton wrappers. Bring the corners of each wrapper into the centre over the filling, folding the sides over each other, and press to seal well. Chill while you make the chowder.

Peel and finely chop the onion. Trim the leeks, cut them lengthwise in half and wash thoroughly, then slice across very finely. Peel the garlic and chop to a paste (see page 13).

Heat the oil and two-thirds of the butter in a saucepan over low heat and cook the onion until soft and translucent, stirring often. Add the garlic and cook gently for 1

minute. Stir in the leeks, sweetcorn and chicken essence. Bring to the boil.

Grate the cheese and add to the pan. Season. Simmer for about 10 minutes or until all the vegetables are tender.

Pour the soup into a food processor and process until as smooth as possible. Strain the soup through a fine sieve into a clean pan, pressing down on the solids in the sieve to extract the maximum flavour and liquid. Leave to reheat gently.

Bring a pan of seasoned chicken essence or salted water to a simmer. Add the wontons and poach gently for 4 minutes; then drain them well.

While the wontons are poaching, pull the stalks from the spinach or sorrel leaves. Wash the leaves thoroughly and pat dry, then stack them and cut across into fine shreds. Heat the remaining butter in a small frying pan and toss the spinach for about 15 seconds or until just wilted.

Divide the spinach among the warmed bowls. Taste and adjust the seasoning of the chowder, then ladle it into the bowls. Add the wontons and serve.

OVER PAGE
Vegetable Soup with Basil and Goat's Cheese Dumplings and Sweetcorn Chowder with Shellfish Wontons

LAMB BROTH WITH BASIL CROÛTES

Serves 4

2 kg / 4¹/₂ lb lamb bones
salt and freshly ground black pepper
1 onion
1 leek, white and pale green parts only
1 carrot
1 large celery stalk
1 garlic clove

5 sprigs of fresh basil
1 sprig of fresh thyme
¹/₂ bay leaf
2 black peppercorns
2 ripe but firm plum tomatoes
12 French Bread Croûtes (see page 31)
2 tbsp freshly grated Parmesan cheese

Trim all fat from the lamb bones, then chop them into pieces (or have your butcher do this for you). Put the bones in a large pot, cover with cold water and bring to the boil. Drain the bones and rinse with cold water. Put them back in the pot, cover with 3 litres / 5 pints / 3 quarts fresh cold water and add some salt. Bring to the boil.

Cut the unpeeled onion in half. Put it cut side down in a small frying pan over moderate heat and brown well. Add the onion to the bones and simmer for about 2 hours, skimming frequently.

Trim the leek, cut it lengthwise in half and wash well, then cut across into thin slices. Peel and chop the carrot. Trim and chop the celery. Peel the garlic clove and cut it in half.

Add the leek, carrot, celery and garlic to the lamb bones. Pull the stalks from the basil leaves; set the leaves aside. Add the stalks to the pot with the thyme and bay leaf. Roughly crush the peppercorns with the base of a small heavy pan and add to the pot.

Peel the tomatoes and remove the seeds (see page 74). Cut the flesh into fine dice and set aside. Add the tomato skins and seeds to the pot. Simmer for a further 45 minutes, skimming often.

Remove and discard the lamb bones.

Strain the broth through a fine sieve or strainer lined with muslin [US cheesecloth] into a clean saucepan. Use paper towels to remove any remaining fat from the surface of the broth.

Taste the broth. If it is not strong enough in flavour, simmer briskly to reduce and concentrate it. Set aside.

Cut the basil leaves into very fine strips and mix with the diced tomatoes. Season with salt and pepper.

Heat the grill [US broiler].

Bring the lamb broth to the boil. Taste and adjust the seasoning.

Pile the tomato mixture on the croûtes and sprinkle with the Parmesan. Grill until the tops are glazed and golden brown.

Surround with the basil croûtes and ladle the lamb broth into the plates. Serve immediately.

TIPS

TIPS

The broth can also be made with beef or chicken bones.

The broth can be served with a small egg custard placed in the middle of each soup plate, with the broth ladled over the top.

TO MAKE EGG CUSTARD

In a bowl mix together 100 ml / 3¹/₂ fl oz / 7 tbsp single cream [US light whipping cream], 1 egg, 1 egg yolk and a pinch of nutmeg. Season, then strain. Butter 4 moulds such as egg cups, 3 tbsp capacity. Pour in the mixture. Set the moulds in a pan of simmering water (to come halfway up the sides of the moulds). Cover and steam for 25–30 minutes or until the custard is just set. Remove from the pan and set aside for 5 minutes before turning out into individual soup plates.

FISH BROTH WITH SAFFRON AND GARLIC MAYONNAISE

Serves 4

The garlic mayonnaise here is a simple version of the French 'rouille'.

1 onion
1 fennel bulb with feathery top
1 leek, white and pale green parts only
2 carrots
2 tbsp olive oil
100 ml / 3 1/2 fl oz / 7 tbsp dry white wine
600 ml / 1 pint / 2 1/2 cups Mussel Essence
  (see page 13)
400 ml / 14 fl oz / 1 3/4 cups Chicken Essence
  (see page 14)
a small pinch of saffron
30 g / 1 oz vermicelli

225 g / 8 oz mixed prepared fish and
  shellfish (see tip)
sea salt and freshly ground black pepper
French Bread Croûtes (see page 31)

For the garlic mayonnaise
100 ml / 3 1/2 fl oz / 7 tbsp dry white wine
2 pinches of saffron
200 ml / 7 fl oz / 7/8 cup Mayonnaise
  (see page 22)
2 garlic cloves

First make the garlic mayonnaise. Put the wine and saffron in a small pan, bring to the boil and simmer until reduced by half. Leave to cool, then strain and mix with the mayonnaise. Peel the garlic and chop to a paste (see page 13). Stir into the mayonnaise. Set aside.

Peel and finely chop the onion. Pull the feathery leaves from the fennel bulb and reserve them. Trim the fennel bulb. Trim the leek, cut it lengthwise in half and wash well. Peel the carrots. Cut the fennel, leek and carrots into 5-mm / 1/4-inch dice.

Heat the oil in a large saucepan over low heat and cook the onion until soft and translucent, stirring often. Add the diced vegetables and cook gently for 1 minute longer.

Add the wine and bring to the boil. Boil until reduced by half. Stir in the mussel and chicken essences and the saffron and bring back to the boil. Simmer until the vegetables are tender.

Meanwhile, drop the vermicelli into a separate pan of boiling salted water and cook until just tender (*al dente*). Drain, rinse with cold running water and drain again well. Set aside.

Season the fish and shellfish with salt and pepper. Add them individually to the broth according to how long they need to be cooked, if at all.

Add the vermicelli to the broth. Taste and adjust the seasoning. Serve the broth garnished with the reserved fennel leaves, with the garlic mayonnaise and French bread croûtes on the side. To serve, stir a spoonful of garlic mayonnaise into each bowl of soup, or spread the mayonnaise on the croûtes and add to the soup.

CREAM OF SPINACH AND OYSTER SOUP

Serves 4

1 large onion
1 small garlic clove
1 celery stalk
100 g / 3¹/₂ oz leeks, white and pale green
    parts only
200 g / 7 oz fresh spinach
15 g / ¹/₂ oz / 1 tbsp unsalted butter

1 tbsp vegetable oil
200 ml / 7 fl oz / ⁷/₈ cup dry white wine
1 litre / 1³/₄ pints / 1 quart Chicken Essence
    (see page 14)
4 fresh oysters in shell
200 ml / 7 fl oz / ⁷/₈ cup cream
salt and freshly ground black pepper

TIP
For oysters to be cooked, as here, I would suggest you use Pacific oysters.

Peel and finely chop the onion. Peel the garlic and chop it to a paste (see page 13). Chop the celery. Trim the leeks, cut them lengthwise in half and wash them well, then chop them. Pull the spinach stalks from the leaves; set the leaves aside.

Heat the butter and oil in a saucepan over low heat and cook the onion until soft and translucent, stirring often. Add the garlic and cook for 1 minute longer.

Add the celery, leeks and spinach stalks and stir well. Cover the pan and cook gently for 5 minutes, stirring occasionally.

Pour in two-thirds of the wine and all the chicken essence and bring to the boil. Simmer, uncovered, for 30 minutes.

Meanwhile, roughly chop the spinach leaves. Open the oysters (see box).

Add the spinach leaves to the soup and simmer for a further 5 minutes.

Purée the soup in a blender or food processor, then press it through a sieve into a clean saucepan. Stir in the cream. Season.

Reheat the soup over very low heat.

Meanwhile, combine the oysters and their liquor with the remaining wine in a saucepan. Poach over low heat for about 10 seconds or just until the edges of the oysters start to curl.

Add the oysters and liquid to the soup and stir well. Taste and adjust the seasoning, then serve immediately.

TO OPEN AN OYSTER

Wearing an oven glove [US oven mitt] or protecting your hand with a folded kitchen cloth, grasp the oyster firmly. Push the side of an oyster knife into the hinge of the oyster shell and twist the knife to open the shell; discard the top shell. Slip the knife under the oyster to release it from the bottom shell. If the oyster is to be cooked (as here), tip it and all the liquor from the shell into a bowl. Pull off the beard and the small, round, hard muscle from the oyster before using.

RIGHT
Cream of Spinach and Oyster Soup

LENTIL SOUP WITH SMOKED DUCK

Serves 4

200 g / 7 oz / 1 cup lentils, preferably from
   Le Puy
1 onion
¹/₂ large carrot
¹/₂ leek, white and pale green parts only
1 celery stalk
2 garlic cloves
3 slices of streaky bacon, preferably smoked
   [US Canadian bacon]

2 tbsp groundnut oil [US peanut oil]
2 tbsp sherry vinegar
1.2 litres / 2 pints / 5 cups Chicken Essence
   (see page 14)
3–4 sprigs of fresh marjoram
salt and freshly ground black pepper
4 tbsp crème fraîche or double cream
   [US heavy whipping cream]
60 g / 2 oz smoked boneless duck breast

TIPS

You can use smoked chicken, turkey or goose instead of duck.

The greeny-blue-tinged lentils from Le Puy are the best ones to use for this soup because their flavour is more intense than other lentils.

Rinse the lentils and pick them over to remove any stones, if necessary. Put the lentils in a bowl, cover with cold water and set aside to soak for at least 2 hours. Change the soaking water once or twice.

Peel and chop the onion and carrot. Trim the leek, cut it lengthwise in half and wash well, then cut across into thin slices. Trim and chop the celery. Peel the garlic and chop to a paste (see page 13). Remove any rind from the bacon and cut it across into fine strips.

Heat the oil in a heavy-based saucepan over low heat and cook all the prepared vegetables and bacon for 5 minutes, stirring often. Drain the lentils and add them to the pan. Add the sherry vinegar and stir until it is almost completely evaporated.

Add the chicken essence and marjoram. Season with salt and pepper. Bring to the boil, then reduce the heat and simmer for 40 minutes.

With a slotted spoon, remove 4 heaped tbsp of the lentils and set them aside. Purée the soup in a food processor or blender, then push it through a sieve into a clean saucepan, pressing down on the solids in the sieve to extract maximum liquid and flavour. Stir in the reserved whole lentils and the cream and reheat gently. Taste and adjust the seasoning.

Remove any excess fat from the duck breast. Cut the breast into thin slices and divide among warmed soup plates. Ladle the soup into the plates and serve.

PARSLEY AND GARLIC SOUP

Serves 4

Use the new season's garlic for this soup, if available.

15 very fresh garlic cloves
1 onion
1 leek, white and pale green parts only
1 celery stalk
75 g / 2¹/₂ oz / 1¹/₄ cups fresh parsley
2 tbsp groundnut oil [US peanut oil]
1 litre / 1³/₄ pints / 1 quart Chicken Essence
*   (see page 14)*

2–3 fresh sage leaves
100 ml / 3¹/₂ fl oz / 7 tbsp crème fraîche or
*   double cream [US heavy whipping cream]*
salt and freshly ground black pepper
60 g / 2 oz Emmenthal cheese
12 French Bread Croûtes (see page 31)

Peel the garlic cloves. Drop them into a pan of boiling water and simmer for 1 minute. Drain and refresh in cold water, then drain again.

Peel and chop the onion. Trim the leek, cut it lengthwise in half and wash well, then cut across into thin slices. Trim and chop the celery. Pull the parsley stalks from the curly sprigs; set the sprigs aside.

Heat the oil in a heavy-based saucepan over a low heat and cook the onion, leek and celery with the parsley stalks until soft, stirring often. Add the garlic cloves and cook gently for 1 minute longer.

Pour in the chicken essence and bring to the boil, then reduce the heat and simmer for 20 minutes.

Chop enough of the parsley sprigs to make 3 tbsp and set aside. Add the remaining parsley sprigs and the sage leaves to the soup and simmer for a further 1 minute. Purée the soup in a blender or food processor, then press it through a fine sieve into a clean saucepan. Stir in the cream, and taste and adjust the seasoning.

Heat the grill [US broiler]. Grate the cheese and mix it with the reserved chopped parsley. Spread this mixture on the croûtes and grill until the cheese has melted and is golden brown. Reheat the soup gently.

Serve the soup hot, with the cheese croûtes.

COLD CUCUMBER AND MINT SOUP WITH HOT SCAMPI

Serves 4

600 g / 1 1/4 lb cucumbers
1 large onion
30 g / 1 oz / 2 tbsp unsalted butter
2 tbsp vegetable oil
14 sprigs of fresh mint
salt and freshly ground black pepper
1 litre / 1 3/4 pints / 1 quart Chicken Essence
   (see page 14)

100 ml / 3 1/2 fl oz / 7 tbsp Greek yogurt or
   other thick plain yogurt
4 tbsp crème fraîche or double cream
   [US heavy whipping cream]
12 raw scampi tails (Dublin Bay prawns)

Peel the cucumbers, cut them in half and scoop out the seeds with a teaspoon. Reserve a 5-cm / 2-inch piece and cut the rest of the cucumber across into thin slices.

Peel and chop the onion. Heat half of the butter and oil in a saucepan over low heat and cook the onion until soft and translucent, stirring often.

Set aside 4 mint sprigs for garnish. Pull the leaves from the remaining stalks and reserve them. Add the mint stalks to the pan together with the cucumber slices. Season with salt and pepper. Add the chicken essence and bring to the boil, reduce the heat and simmer for 10–15 minutes or until the cucumbers are very soft.

Discard the mint stalks, then purée the soup in a blender or food processor. Pass the soup through a fine sieve into a bowl. Leave to cool, then stir in the yogurt and the cream.

Cut the reserved cucumber into small dice. Chop the mint leaves. Stir the diced cucumber and chopped mint into the cold soup. Taste and adjust the seasoning. Ladle the soup into chilled soup plates.

Peel the scampi if necessary, then dry with paper towels and season with salt and pepper. Heat the remaining butter and oil in a frying pan over a high heat and fry the scampi for 2–3 minutes or until they are opaque and golden brown on both sides. Drain on paper towels.

Place the hot scampi in the middle of the bowls of soup, garnish with the reserved mint sprigs and serve immediately.

TIPS
Raw tiger or king prawns [US jumbo shrimp] can be used in place of the scampi. After peeling them, make a shallow cut down the rounded back of each and remove the dark intestinal vein.

Always adjust the seasoning of a cold dish when it has reached serving temperature. Cold food needs more seasoning than food served hot or lukewarm.

RIGHT
Cold Cucumber and Mint Soup with Hot Scampi

CHILLED BEAN AND PESTO SOUP WITH RED PEPPER

Serves 4-6

225 g / 8 oz / 1 1/4 cups dried butter beans
  [US dried Fordhook lima beans]
1 onion
3 garlic cloves
3 tbsp olive oil
50 g / 1 2/3 oz / 1 loosely packed cup
  fresh basil

3 ripe but firm plum tomatoes
1.2 litres / 2 pints / 5 cups Chicken Essence
  (see page 14)
salt and freshly ground black pepper
200 ml / 7 fl oz / 7/8 cup Pesto Sauce
  (see page 24)
1 red sweet pepper

Wash the beans thoroughly, then cook them in boiling water for 8 minutes. Drain and refresh under cold running water. Squeeze the beans gently in your fingers to slip off the skins.

Peel and finely chop the onion. Peel the garlic and chop to a paste (see page 13). Heat the oil in a large saucepan over low heat and cook the onion until soft and translucent, stirring often. Add two-thirds of the garlic and cook for 1 minute longer.

Meanwhile, remove the basil leaves from the stalks; set the leaves aside. Chop the tomatoes.

Add the basil stalks, tomatoes, beans and chicken essence to the saucepan. Season with salt and pepper. Bring to the boil, then reduce the heat and simmer for 25 minutes or until the beans are very tender.

Stir in the basil leaves and the remaining garlic and simmer for a further 5 minutes. Remove from the heat and allow to cool.

Purée the soup in a blender or food processor. Stir in the pesto sauce. Press the soup through a fine sieve into a bowl. Taste and adjust the seasoning, then cover and chill for at least 2 hours.

Heat the grill [US broiler]. Roast the red pepper under the grill until the skin is charred on all sides. Alternatively, impale the pepper on a long-handled fork and turn it in a gas flame to char the skin all over. Put the pepper in a plastic bag and set aside to cool until it can be handled.

Peel the skin from the pepper. Discard the stalk and white ribs and cut the flesh into very fine matchsticks.

Add the red pepper to the soup just before serving.

Pumpkin Soup with Liver Dumplings

Serves 4-6

TIP

The liver dumplings can also be served as a main dish. Double the quantities and make the dumplings twice the size, poaching them for about 8 minutes. Olive oil potatoes (see recipe on page 141) would be an excellent accompaniment, as would sauerkraut.

1 large onion
100 g / 3½ oz leek, white and pale green parts only
1-kg / 2¼-lb piece of pumpkin
2 garlic cloves
1-cm / ½-inch piece of fresh root ginger
15 g / ½ oz / 1 tbsp unsalted butter
1 tbsp groundnut oil [US peanut oil]
10 sprigs of fresh coriander [US cilantro]
250 ml / 8 fl oz / 1 cup milk
salt and freshly ground black pepper
100 ml / 3½ fl oz / 7 tbsp Greek yogurt or other thick plain yogurt

For the liver dumplings
½ small onion
1 small garlic clove
15 g / ½ oz / 1 tbsp unsalted butter
1 tsp vegetable oil
2 bread rolls
a little milk
150 g / 5 oz calf's liver
1 tbsp chopped fresh parsley
a pinch of freshly grated nutmeg
1 egg and 1 egg yolk
about 500 ml / 16 fl oz / 2 cups Chicken Essence (see page 14)

Make the dumpling mixture. Peel and chop the onion. Peel the garlic and chop to a paste (see page 13). Heat the butter and oil in a pan and cook the onion until soft. Add the garlic and cook for 1 minute longer. Cut the bread rolls into slices, cover with milk and soak for 5 minutes. Cut the liver into cubes and dry on paper towels.

Squeeze the bread to remove excess milk. Combine the bread, liver and onion mixture and pass through the fine plate/disc of a mincer [US meat grinder], or you can use a food processor. Mix in the parsley and season. Work in the whole egg and egg yolk. Chill for at least 1½ hours.

Bring the chicken essence to the boil in a wide pan, then simmer. To shape each dumpling, take a dessertspoon (2 tsp capacity) of the liver mixture. Lower gently into the essence. Leave the spoon in the liquid until the dumpling comes away. Poach the dumplings for 5 minutes. With a slotted spoon, transfer the dumplings to a bowl. Ladle a little of the essence over them and set aside. Strain the remaining chicken essence and check the quantity; if

necessary, add more essence to make it up to 500 ml / 16 fl oz / 2 cups again. Set aside.

To make the soup, peel and chop the onion. Trim the leek, cut it lengthwise and wash well, then slice across thinly. Peel the pumpkin, discard the seeds and fibres, and chop the flesh. Peel the garlic and chop to a paste. Peel and finely chop the ginger.

Heat the butter and oil in a saucepan and cook the onion until soft, stirring often. Add the leek and cook for 2 minutes. Add the garlic and ginger to the pan and cook for 1 minute longer.

Pull the coriander leaves from the stalks and reserve. Add the stalks to the pan with the pumpkin, chicken essence and milk. Season. Bring to the boil, then reduce the heat, cover and simmer for about 20 minutes, stirring frequently.

Discard the coriander stalks and stir the yogurt into the soup. Purée the soup in a food processor, then pass it through a fine sieve into a saucepan. Adjust the seasoning. Drain the dumplings and add to the soup. Reheat without boiling. Serve hot, sprinkled with chopped coriander leaves.

ANTON EDELMANN CREATIVE CUISINE

CREAM OF CRAB SOUP WITH CRAB TOASTS

Serves 4

1 live crab, weighing about 1 kg / 2¼ lb
1 large onion
2 garlic cloves
1 celery stalk
1 leek, white and pale green parts only
4 sprigs of fresh coriander [US cilantro]
3 tbsp groundnut oil [US peanut oil]
1 sprig of fresh thyme
6 tbsp port wine
1.75 litres / 3 pints / 7 cups Chicken Essence
   (see page 14)
30 g / 1 oz Cheddar cheese

45 g / 1½ oz / 3 tbsp unsalted butter
45 g / 1½ oz / 4 tbsp flour
salt and freshly ground black pepper
4 tbsp crème fraîche or double cream
   [US heavy whipping cream]

For the crab toasts
3 tbsp Mayonnaise (see page 22)
¼ tsp Worcestershire sauce
3 drops of Tabasco sauce
4 slices of hot toast

Immerse the crab in a saucepan of boiling salted water and simmer for 15 minutes.

Peel and chop the onion and garlic. Chop the celery. Trim the leek, cut it lengthwise and wash, then chop it. Pull the coriander stalks from the leaves; set the leaves aside.

Drain the crab and allow to cool. Twist off the legs and claws and pull the body and shell apart. Discard the stomach sac and any green matter just below the head. Discard the pale grey fronds. Remove all the brown and white meat from the shell, keeping them separate. Crack the claws and remove the meat; discard any cartilage.

Put all the shells in a heavy-duty plastic bag inside a towel and pound with a rolling pin or pan until crushed as finely as possible.

Heat the oil in a saucepan and fry the crab shells over moderately high heat for 5 minutes, stirring frequently. Do not let them brown too much. Add the onion, garlic, leek, celery, coriander stalks and thyme and stir well. Cover and cook for a further 5 minutes, stirring occasionally.

Pour in the port and chicken essence and bring to the boil. Cover and simmer for 30 minutes.

Strain the crab broth through a fine sieve or strainer lined with muslin [US cheesecloth], pressing down on the shells and vegetables to extract the maximum flavour and liquid. Allow the broth to cool.

Grate the cheese. Chop the coriander leaves. Melt the butter in a saucepan over low heat. Stir in the flour and cook for 2 minutes, stirring constantly. This mixture should not brown at all. Gradually stir in the cold crab broth and then the cheese and half the brown meat from the crab. Season with salt and pepper. Bring to the boil, stirring frequently, and simmer for 10 minutes.

Meanwhile, make the crab toasts. Mix the remaining brown meat from the crab and the mayonnaise in a food processor. Season to taste with Worcestershire sauce, Tabasco sauce, salt and pepper. Spread the mixture on the hot toast and cut each slice into squares.

Strain the soup through a fine sieve. Taste and adjust the seasoning, then ladle it into warmed bowls. Garnish with white crab meat and the chopped coriander and serve with the crab toasts.

TIPS

The wonderful flavour of this soup comes from the crab shells. The white meat from the crab is used as a garnish, and the brown meat to top the accompanying toasts. Any extra white crab meat can be enjoyed in a sandwich.

Lobster or langoustines can be used instead of crab. The crab toasts can be replaced by garlic croûtes (see recipe on page 31).

FIRST COURSES

A LOT of thought should go into choosing and preparing a first course because it is the springboard to the exciting things to follow. It should be teasing to the taste buds. It should please the eyes. It should not be too strong in flavour or over-spiced. It must be in contrast to what is to follow, in terms of texture, colour and taste. And it should only be just enough to stimulate the appetite.

Try to keep it seasonal (this is true for all food, of course) so that the ingredients will be at their freshest, with their fullest flavour. Even though almost every vegetable, fruit and berry is available all year round, the excitement of eating the first locally grown asparagus or the first new potato of the season is always a revelation and wonderful surprise.

SPINACH AND POTATO OMELETTE WITH FETA CHEESE

Serves 4

225 g / 8 oz potatoes
100 g / 3 1/2 oz fresh spinach leaves
2 ripe but firm plum tomatoes
6 tbsp olive oil

12 eggs
200 g / 7 oz feta cheese
salt and freshly ground black pepper

Peel the potatoes and cut them into 5-mm / 1/4-inch cubes. Rinse them well to remove excess starch, then dry on paper towels.

Blanch the spinach in boiling water for 30 seconds. Drain and refresh under cold running water, then drain and squeeze well to remove all excess liquid. Chop the spinach roughly.

Peel the tomatoes and remove the seeds (see page 74). Cut the tomato flesh into small dice.

Heat 2 tbsp olive oil in a large frying pan over a moderate heat. Add the potatoes and fry them until they are tender. Do not let them become crisp or colour too much.

Meanwhile, put the eggs in a bowl and lightly beat them to mix. Add the spinach and tomatoes. Crumble the feta into the bowl. Season with salt and pepper.

Heat 1 tbsp oil in a 20-cm / 8-inch omelette pan over high heat. Add one-quarter of the potatoes and one-quarter of the egg mixture and cook for 30 seconds. Lower the heat to moderate and continue cooking for about 3 minutes, stirring often with a fork and lifting the set edges to let the liquid egg run on to the pan. When ready, the omelette will be firm but still slightly soft in the centre (it will continue to cook in its own heat after you remove it from the pan).

Slide the omelette out on to a warmed plate. Make 3 more omelettes in the same way. Serve hot.

TIP
If you prefer, you can make one large omelette and cut it into quarters for serving.

LENTIL RAGOÛT
WITH SOFT-BOILED EGGS

Serves 4

300 g / 10 oz / 2 cups lentils, preferably from Le Puy
1 small onion
1/2 garlic clove
1/2 small carrot
1/2 small leek, white and pale green parts only
60 g / 2 oz button mushrooms
2 tbsp groundnut oil [US peanut oil]
15 g / 1/2 oz / 1 tbsp unsalted butter
300 ml / 1/2 pint / 11/4 cups port wine
400 ml / 14 fl oz / 13/4 cups Chicken Concentrate (see page 16)
salt and freshly ground black pepper
4 slices of smoked bacon [US Canadian bacon]
4 eggs
Croûtons (see box), to finish

Rinse the lentils thoroughly under cold running water and pick them over to remove any stones if necessary. Add them to a pan of boiling salted water and simmer for 30–35 minutes or until they are nearly done.

Meanwhile, peel and finely chop the onion. Peel the garlic and chop it to a paste (see page 13). Peel and finely dice the carrot. Cut the leek in half and wash well, then chop finely. Trim off the mushroom stalks and cut the caps into quarters.

Heat the oil and butter in a large saucepan over low heat and cook the onion until soft and translucent, stirring often. Add the garlic and cook gently for 1 minute longer. Stir in the carrot, leek and mushrooms, cover the pan and cook until the vegetables are soft.

Add the port and bring to the boil. Boil, uncovered, until reduced by two-thirds.

Drain the lentils and add them to the vegetables together with the chicken concentrate. Season with salt and pepper. Simmer for 15–20 minutes or until the liquid is reduced and the ragoût has a fairly thick consistency. Stir occasionally, and then more frequently towards the end as the ragoût thickens.

While the ragoût is simmering, prepare the bacon and eggs. Heat the grill [US broiler]. Grill the bacon until it is crisp and browned, turning once. Drain on paper towels, then cut the slices across into thin strips. Add to the ragoût.

Put the eggs into a saucepan of simmering water and cook for 4 minutes. Drain and rinse with cold water. When the eggs are cool enough to handle, peel off the shells. Reheat the eggs in simmering salted water for 2 minutes, then drain and dry on paper towels.

Taste the lentil ragoût and adjust the seasoning, then divide among warmed plates. Place an egg on top of each serving and sprinkle with croûtons. Serve immediately.

TO MAKE CROÛTONS
Take 4 slices of white bread, 5-mm / 1/4-inch. Cut the slices into cubes. Spread the cubes on a baking sheet and toast in the oven for 5-6 minutes or until crisp and golden brown all over, stirring and tossing occasionally.

POACHED EGGS ON CREAMED SMOKED HADDOCK WITH BLACK PUDDING

Serves 4

This could also serve 2 for lunch or for what our American cousins call brunch.

100 ml / 3¹/₂ fl oz / 7 tbsp white wine vinegar
4 eggs
175 ml / 6 fl oz / ³/₄ cup double cream
  [US heavy whipping cream]
300 ml / ¹/₂ pint / 1¹/₄ cups milk
200 g / 7 oz skinless smoked haddock fillet
  [US finnan haddie]

freshly ground black pepper
16 slices of black pudding [US blood
  sausage], 1-cm / ¹/₂-inch thick, weighing
  about 180 g / 6 oz
Sauté Potatoes (see page 140), to serve

Put 1 litre / 1³/₄ pints / 1 US quart of water and the vinegar in a deep saucepan and bring to the boil. Reduce the heat so the water is just simmering. Crack each egg into a cup, then slide it gently into the simmering water. Cook for about 3 minutes or until all the egg white has closed and set around the yolk. Lift the eggs out of the water and slide them into a bowl of cold water (this will stop them cooking and will also wash off the taste of the vinegar). Drain on paper towels. Trim off any straggly bits and set the eggs aside, covered.

Reserve 4 tbsp of the cream and put the remainder in a saucepan with the milk. Bring the liquid to a simmer. Add the smoked haddock and poach for 2 minutes or until the fish will just flake easily when tested with a fork.

Heat the grill [US broiler].

Remove the fish with a slotted spoon and set it aside to cool slightly. Boil the poaching liquid until it is very thick and reduced by about two-thirds. Flake the haddock, removing any bones, and mix with 4 tbsp of the reduced liquid. Season lightly with pepper.

Grill the slices of black pudding for about 1¹/₂ minutes on each side or until slightly crisp. Heat the poached eggs in a pan of gently simmering salted water for about 2 minutes. Heat the reserved 4 tbsp of cream in a small pan.

Spoon the creamed haddock in a mound in the centre of each warmed plate. Drain the eggs on paper towels and set on top of the haddock. Spoon 1 tbsp hot cream on to each egg. Arrange the slices of black pudding and the sauté potatoes around the edge and serve.

TIPS

When poaching eggs, never add salt to the water because it stops the egg white from closing properly around the yolks. If you use a tall pan with lots of liquid in it, the eggs will have a nice round shape. Once poached, the eggs can be kept in water in the refrigerator for up to 2 days.

Although smoked haddock was the inspiration for this dish, you could also use kippers, smoked halibut or smoked salmon.

The quality of the black pudding is of paramount importance.

RIGHT
Poached Eggs on Creamed Smoked Haddock with Black Pudding

TORTELLINI WITH SAGE

Serves 4

These tortellini, filled with braised veal, Parma ham and spinach, are delicious, and it is worth making a good batch of them at one time so you can cook some right away and have more on hand in the refrigerator or freezer for another meal. The quantities of filling and pasta dough here will make about 72 tortellini, weighing about 450 g / 1 lb. The sauce and garnish quantities are for 4. If you want to serve more, it is easy to increase them.

350 g / 12 oz *Pasta Dough (see page 26)*
1 egg
1 1/2 tbsp olive oil
4 tbsp freshly grated Parmesan cheese
45 g / 1 1/2 oz / 3 tbsp unsalted butter
8 fresh sage leaves

For the filling
200 g / 7 oz boneless pie veal [US stewing veal]
1 onion
3 garlic cloves
2 tbsp olive oil
125 ml / 4 fl oz / 1/2 cup dry white wine
125 ml / 4 fl oz / 1/2 cup Chicken Concentrate (see page 16)

30 g / 1 oz Parmesan cheese
30 g / 1 oz Parma ham
60 g / 2 oz fresh spinach leaves
45 g / 1 1/2 oz / 3 tbsp unsalted butter
3 sprigs of fresh sage
3 sprigs of fresh rosemary
salt and freshly ground black pepper

For the sauce (to serve 4)
2 shallots
1 small garlic clove
2 ripe but firm plum tomatoes
45 g / 1 1/2 oz small button mushrooms
1 1/2 tbsp olive oil
4 tbsp dry white wine
4 tbsp Chicken Concentrate (see page 16)

First make the filling. Heat the oven to 170°C / 325°F / gas 3. Cut the veal into small cubes. Peel and finely chop the onion. Peel the garlic and chop to a paste (see page 13).

Heat a small flameproof casserole over high heat and add the oil. Season the cubes of veal and fry them quickly to seal them. Remove with a slotted spoon.

Add the onion to the casserole and cook over low heat until soft and translucent, stirring often. Add the garlic and cook gently for 1 minute longer. Return the veal to the casserole and stir in the wine. Bring to the boil, then reduce the heat and simmer until reduced by half.

Add the chicken concentrate and stir well, then cover the casserole and transfer it to the oven. Braise for 45–60 minutes or until the veal is very tender. Stir from time to time.

Meanwhile, grate the Parmesan and set it aside. Coarsely chop the Parma ham.

Add the ham to the casserole. Cover again and cook for a further 10 minutes.

Pull any stalks from the spinach, then wash thoroughly. Blanch in boiling water for about 1 minute. Drain and, when cool enough to handle, squeeze to remove all excess water. Add the spinach to the meat mixture and allow to cool.

Pass the mixture through the fine

plate/disc of a mincer [US meat grinder], or purée it in a food processor.

Melt the butter in the frying pan and add the herbs. Cook, swirling the butter around in the pan, until it is lightly browned. Strain the herb-flavoured butter into the meat mixture; discard the herbs. Stir in the Parmesan and season with salt and pepper.

Using a pasta machine on the narrowest setting, roll out the pasta dough. Cut into 6-cm / 2¼-inch squares. Dust the squares lightly with flour, then cover with cling film [US plastic wrap] so they do not dry out.

Lightly beat the egg. Brush around the edge of a pasta square and spoon a little filling into the centre. Fold over in half to form a triangle and press the edges to seal. Roll over again in the same direction, then bring the 2 outside points together over the centre, put a little egg on them and press them to seal. Continue making the tortellini in this way, spreading them out on a baking sheet or tray. Cover and refrigerate until ready to cook.

To make the sauce, peel and finely chop the shallots. Peel the garlic and chop to a paste (see page 13). Peel the tomatoes and remove the seeds (see page 74), then cut the flesh into fine dice. Trim the mushroom stalks, then slice the mushrooms.

Heat the oil in a saucepan over low heat and cook the shallots until soft and translucent, stirring often. Add the garlic and cook for 1 minute longer. Add the mushrooms and cook, stirring, until they have given up their liquid. Stir in the tomato dice and white wine and bring to the boil. Simmer until the liquid has reduced by three-quarters. Stir in the chicken concentrate and season with salt and pepper. Keep the sauce warm.

Heat the grill [US broiler].

Cook the tortellini in a large pan of boiling salted water for about 2 minutes or until the pasta is tender but still firm (*al dente*). Drain well and toss with the olive oil.

Spoon the sauce into individual gratin dishes or flameproof soup plates and spread it out evenly. Place the tortellini on top and sprinkle with the Parmesan. Heat under the grill until the top is glazed and golden brown.

Meanwhile, melt the butter in a small pan and add the sage leaves. Cook, swirling the butter around in the pan, until it is lightly browned.

Put 2 sage leaves on each serving and dribble over the browned butter. Serve immediately.

ASPARAGUS WITH QUAIL'S EGGS AND HERB DRESSING

Serves 4

To my mind, there can be nothing finer than fresh asparagus in season served with softly boiled quail's eggs and a simple dressing. The flavours are intense and pleasing.

12 quail's eggs
2 ripe but firm plum tomatoes
32 asparagus spears, weighing about
    1 kg / 2¼ lb
fresh chervil leaves, to garnish

For the egg and herb dressing
1 tbsp balsamic vinegar
1 tbsp white wine vinegar
100 ml / 3½ fl oz / 7 tbsp olive oil
½ tsp soy sauce
salt and freshly ground black pepper
1 hard-boiled egg
1 tbsp chopped mixed fresh herbs such as
    chervil, coriander [US cilantro] and
    flat-leaf (Italian) parsley

Cook the quail's eggs in boiling water for 1 minute. Drain and refresh under cold running water, then peel carefully. Set aside in a bowl of cold water.

Peel the tomatoes and remove the seeds (see page 74). Cut the tomato flesh neatly into small dice and set aside.

For the dressing, mix together the vinegars, oil and soy sauce. Season to taste with salt and pepper. Chop the hard-boiled egg very finely and reserve.

Prepare the asparagus (see page 90). Tie the asparagus into bundles of 8 spears each and trim the ends so the spears are all the same length. Cook in boiling salted water for about 6 minutes or until just tender but still firm. Drain well, then refresh briefly in iced water. Pat dry with paper towels.

While the asparagus is cooking, warm the quail's eggs in a little hot salted water for 1 minute. Dry on paper towels.

Arrange 8 asparagus spears on each warmed plate in the shape of a fan. Sprinkle with the diced tomatoes. Place the quail's eggs on the asparagus. Stir the chopped hard-boiled egg and herbs into the dressing, then spoon a little of the dressing over the quail's eggs and asparagus. Garnish with chervil leaves and serve immediately.

RIGHT
Asparagus with Quail's
Eggs and Herb Dressing

GRILLED SCALLOPS ON YOUNG LEEKS

Serves 4

The cream of leeks can be served as a vegetable with other dishes.

700 g / 1¹/₂ lb baby leeks, white and pale
  green parts only
500 ml / 16 fl oz / 2 cups Chicken Essence
  (see page 14)
sea salt and freshly ground black pepper
8 scallops [US sea scallops], weighing about
  400 g / 14 oz

3 ripe but firm plum tomatoes
200 ml / 7 fl oz / ⁷/₈ cup double cream
  [US heavy whipping cream]
2–3 tbsp vegetable oil
1 tbsp chopped fresh chives

Trim the leeks, and cut diagonally into 7-cm / 2³/₄-inch pieces. Wash well. Put the leeks and chicken essence in a saucepan and season with salt and pepper. Bring to the boil and simmer for 5 minutes or until the leeks are tender but not mushy.

Meanwhile, trim the hard, greyish-white gristly bit from each scallop, leaving just the tender white nut of meat. Cut the scallops in half horizontally. Put them in a bowl of iced water and leave for 10 minutes to firm up.

Peel the tomatoes and remove the seeds (see page 74). Cut the tomato flesh into neat dice.

Drain the leeks, reserving the essence, and refresh them in iced water. Drain again well and set aside on paper towels to dry.

Return 200 ml / 7 fl oz / ⁷/₈ cup of the

essence to the pan and boil until reduced by three-quarters. Stir in the cream and boil again until reduced by half.

Heat a ridged cast-iron grill pan, or the grill [US broiler] and the grill pan with rack in place.

Drain the scallops and dry well with paper towels. Season with salt and pepper and turn in the oil to coat. Arrange on the hot cast-iron pan or on the hot rack under the grill and cook for about 2 minutes on each side.

Meanwhile, add the leeks to the cream sauce and heat through. Stir in the tomato dice, and taste and adjust the seasoning.

Spoon the creamed leeks on to warmed plates and arrange the scallops on top. Sprinkle with the chives and serve.

TIP
Use freshly ground black pepper generously in this dish.

TIGER PRAWNS IN FILO WITH MANGO SAUCE

Serves 4

16 raw tiger prawns [US jumbo shrimp]
sea salt and freshly ground black pepper
16 squares of filo pastry dough,
    each 10 x 10 cm/4 x 4 inches
melted unsalted butter
32 large fresh basil leaves
1 egg yolk
vegetable oil for deep frying
4 handfuls of mixed salad leaves, weighing
    about 90 g / 3 oz
4 tbsp Soy Vinaigrette (see page 21)

For the mango sauce
1 large, ripe mango
1 hard-boiled egg yolk
4 tbsp Mayonnaise (see page 22)
2 tsp finely shredded fresh basil

First make the mango sauce. Peel the mango, then cut the flesh from the flat central stone [US pit]. Chop the flesh coarsely. You should have about 100 g / 3½ oz / ⅔ cup of mango flesh. Put the flesh in a food processor or blender with the hard-boiled egg yolk and mayonnaise and work until smooth. Press the mixture through a fine sieve into a bowl. Stir in the basil and season to taste with salt and pepper. Set the sauce aside.

Peel the prawns, then make a shallow cut down the rounded back of each and remove the dark intestinal vein. Rinse the prawns and pat dry with paper towels. Season with salt and pepper.

Put a filo square on the work surface and brush it with melted butter. Set a basil leaf in the centre and put a prawn on top. Lightly beat the egg yolk and brush a little on the edges of the filo square. Fold 2 opposite sides of the square over the prawn and press to seal. Press the ends together to seal. Wrap and seal the remaining prawns in the same way.

Heat a pan of oil for deep frying to 165–175°C / 330–345°F.

Meanwhile, wash and dry the salad leaves thoroughly .

When the oil is hot, add the prawns in filo, 4 at a time. Fry for 3 minutes or until golden and crisp, turning them over a few times so that they brown evenly. Drain on paper towels. At the end of frying, turn up the heat under the pan until the oil is 180°C / 350°F. Add the remaining basil leaves and fry for a few seconds until crisp, bright green and translucent; drain.

Toss the salad leaves in the soy vinaigrette, then divide among the plates, piling the leaves in a mound at the top. Arrange the prawns in filo in the centre of the plates and garnish with the fried basil. Serve with the mango sauce.

OVER PAGE
Tiger Prawns in Filo with Mango Sauce

SEAFOOD RISOTTO

Serves 4

Risotto makes a lovely light and uncomplicated meal, and the variations are endless.

600 ml / 1 pint / 2¹/₂ cups Mussel Essence
  (see page 13)
1 onion
1 garlic clove
3 tbsp olive oil
120 g / 4 oz / ²/₃ cup risotto rice
100 ml / 3¹/₂ fl oz / 7 tbsp dry white wine

a pinch of saffron
45 g / 1¹/₂ oz / 3 tbsp unsalted butter
450 g / 1 lb prepared seafood, including
  mussels used to make the essence
sea salt and freshly ground black pepper
3 tbsp chopped fresh parsley

Reserve 5 tbsp of the mussel essence. Put the remaining essence in a saucepan and bring it to a simmer.

Peel and finely chop the onion. Peel the garlic and chop to a paste (see page 13). Heat the oil in a wide heavy-based pan over low heat and cook the onion until soft and translucent, stirring often. Add the garlic and cook for 1 minute longer.

Add the rice to the onion and garlic and cook for about 30 seconds, stirring so the grains become coated with oil. Pour in the wine and bring to the boil. Boil until reduced to a glaze, stirring frequently.

Crumble the saffron and stir into the rice. Add a ladleful of the simmering essence, just enough to cover the rice. Cook over moderate heat until it has almost all been absorbed, then add another ladleful of essence. Continue cooking in this way, adding the essence little by little and stirring occasionally. The rice should always be covered by liquid. The total cooking time will be 15–20 minutes.

Meanwhile, if using cubes of fish, heat one-third of the butter in a pan, add the fish and reserved essence, and season with salt and pepper. Cook gently until the fish is just opaque. Remove from the heat and keep warm.

When the rice is nearly done, stir in the remaining butter and season with salt and pepper. Add the mussels with other shellfish if using and heat through briefly. Stir in cubes of fish, with their liquid, and the parsley. Taste and adjust the seasoning, and serve.

TIP

In addition to the mussels used to make the essence, you can add other types of fish or shellfish to the risotto. Fillets of firm fish such as red mullet, sole and monkfish are excellent in a risotto. Leave the skin on red mullet (be sure scales have been removed). Cut the fish into large cubes. You can also use clams, steamed and removed from their shells, and shelled cooked crustaceans such as scampi or Dublin Bay prawns, langoustines, large shrimp or king prawns and lobster. Devein shrimp and prawns and cut lobster into cubes.

RISOTTO VARIATIONS

For a WILD MUSHROOM RISOTTO, use Chicken Essence (see page 14) instead of mussel essence and red wine instead of white, and omit the saffron. Add 175 g / 6 oz fresh wild mushrooms, trimmed, after the garlic and cook for 1 minute before adding the rice. With the butter, stir in 30 g / 1 oz / ¹/₄ cup freshly grated Parmesan cheese.

You can also make many different VEGETABLE RISOTTOS in the same way by adding 175 g / 6 oz prepared vegetables, such as artichoke bottoms, bulb fennel, courgettes [US zucchini], sweet peppers, and cauliflower, instead of wild mushrooms. Use white wine, not red, for this.

TAGLIATELLE WITH MUSSELS, CLAMS AND PESTO

Serves 4-6

400 g / 14 oz *Pasta Dough (see page 26)*
700 g / 1¹/₂ lb *fresh mussels*
700 g / 1¹/₂ lb *fresh venus clams [US small hardshell clams]*
1 *small leek, white and pale green parts only*
1 *celery stalk*
1 *small onion*

300 ml / ¹/₂ pint / 1¹/₄ cups *dry white wine*
300 ml / ¹/₂ pint / 1¹/₄ cups *double cream [US heavy whipping cream]*
5 tbsp *Pesto Sauce (see page 24)*
salt and freshly ground black pepper
3 tbsp *chopped fresh flat-leaf (Italian) parsley*

Using a pasta machine on the second narrowest setting, roll out the pasta dough. Feed the dough through the broad cutting blades on the pasta machine to cut tagliatelle. Dust them with flour and lay out on a clean surface. Leave to dry for about 20 minutes.

Meanwhile, scrub the mussels and clams well under cold running water, and scrape the beards and any barnacles from the mussels. All the shells should be tightly closed, or should close if tapped sharply on the work surface; discard any mussels or clams that remain open or that have cracked or broken shells.

Trim the leek, cut it lengthwise in half and wash well, then slice it finely. Trim and finely slice the celery. Peel and finely chop the onion.

Put half the prepared vegetables in a deep pot and add half the wine and the mussels. Cover and cook over high heat for about 5 minutes or until the mussel shells are all open. Shake the pot frequently. Drain the mussels in a colander set in a bowl. Tip the mussels into another bowl, cover with a kitchen cloth and leave to cool.

Repeat to cook the clams, using the rest of the vegetables and wine. Drain their liquid into the bowl containing the mussel liquid.

Remove the mussels and clams from their shells, working over the bowl containing the cooking liquid so that all the liquor from the shells is retained. Discard any mussels or clams that have remained stubbornly closed. Trim the black-tipped siphon from clams and any remaining beard from the mussels. Set the shellfish aside.

Strain the mussel and clam cooking liquid through a sieve lined with muslin [US cheesecloth]. Pour 200 ml / 7 fl oz / ⁷/₈ cup of the strained liquid into a saucepan. Bring to the boil and boil until reduced by three-quarters.

Add the cream and boil to reduce by half. Meanwhile, bring a large pot of salted water to the boil.

Stir the pesto sauce into the cream and keep hot. Cook the tagliatelle in the boiling salted water for about 2 minutes or until it is just tender but still firm (*al dente*). Drain it well, rinse briefly with cold running water to stop it cooking further, and return to the pot. Add the pesto and cream sauce, the mussels and clams and toss well. Season with salt and pepper.

Serve immediately, sprinkled with the parsley.

GRILLED RED MULLET ON FENNEL WITH SWEET PEPPERS

Serves 4

1 medium-sized fennel bulb
2–3 Chinese leaves [US Napa cabbage leaves]
1 red sweet pepper
1 green sweet pepper
100 g / 3¹/₂ oz / ²/₃ cup whole unsalted
  cashew nuts
4 red mullet fillets, each about 90 g / 3 oz,
  skin scaled

sea salt and freshly ground black pepper
3 tbsp groundnut oil [US peanut oil]
125 ml / 4 fl oz / ¹/₂ cup Red Pepper Pesto
  (see page 24)
4 tsp freshly grated Parmesan cheese
4 tbsp Sherry Vinaigrette (see page 21)

Trim the fennel bulb and discard any bruised outside layers. Cut the bulb lengthwise in half and cut out the core at the bottom in a V-shape. Shred the fennel very finely.

Trim the root end of the Chinese leaves. Wash them well and pat dry. Stack the leaves and cut across into very fine shreds.

Cut the core from the red and green peppers. Cut them in half and discard the seeds and white ribs, then slice very finely.

Heat the grill [US broiler].

Spread the cashew nuts in the grill pan and toast under the grill until you can smell the nuts. Shake the pan occasionally so the nuts toast evenly. Set them aside. Put the rack in the grill pan and heat it.

Season the red mullet fillets with salt and pepper, then turn them in the oil to coat both sides. Arrange skin side down on the hot rack in the grill pan and grill close to the heat for 1 minute. Turn the fillets over and cook for a further 1 minute.

Spread the red pepper pesto evenly over the skin side of the fillets. Sprinkle with the Parmesan. Return to the grill and cook until the cheese and pesto are lightly browned and bubbling.

Meanwhile, toss the fennel, Chinese leaves, red and green peppers and cashew nuts in the vinaigrette.

Divide the vegetable salad among the plates, piling it into a mound in the centre. Set the fillets on top, give them a grind of the peppermill, and serve immediately.

RIGHT
Grilled Red Mullet on Fennel with Sweet Peppers

ASPARAGUS AND GOAT'S CHEESE TART

Serves 4

The slight acid taste of goat's cheese blends perfectly with fresh asparagus.

120 g / 4 oz / 3/4 cup flour
a pinch of salt
50 g / 1²/₃ oz / 4 tbsp unsalted butter
40 g / 1¹/₃ oz / ¹/₄ cup cream cheese
1 egg yolk
1 tsp lemon juice
1–2 tsp iced water

For the filling
1 onion
15 g / ¹/₂ oz / 1 tbsp unsalted butter
10 medium-sized fresh asparagus spears
120 g / 4 oz firm goat's cheese
3 eggs
150 ml / ¹/₄ pint / ²/₃ cup double cream
 [US heavy whipping cream]
salt and freshly ground black pepper

TIPS
If the filling and pastry are browning too quickly towards the end of baking, cover with foil.

At The Savoy, we serve this tart with a little red pepper juice (see page 89) spooned around it.

Sift the flour into a bowl and add the salt. Rub in the butter and cream cheese until thoroughly incorporated. Lightly beat the egg yolk and add to the bowl with the lemon juice. Mix in, adding enough iced water to bind to a smooth, evenly blended dough. Form the dough into a ball, wrap and chill for 15 minutes.

Heat the oven to 200°C / 400°F / gas 6.

Turn the dough on to a lightly floured surface and roll it out thinly. Use to line a 20-cm / 8-inch loose-bottomed flan tin [US tart pan] or flan ring set on a baking sheet, pressing the dough in gently. Chill for 15 minutes.

Meanwhile, peel and finely chop the onion. Melt the butter in a small pan over low heat and cook the onion until soft and translucent, stirring often. Remove from the heat and leave to cool.

Line the pastry case with greaseproof paper [US wax paper] and weigh this down with ceramic baking beans or dried beans. Bake for about 20 minutes.

Meanwhile, prepare the asparagus (see page 90). Cook the asparagus spears in boiling salted water for about 6 minutes or until just tender but still firm. Drain well, then refresh briefly in iced water. Pat dry with paper towels. Cut a 7.5-cm / 3-inch piece from the tip end of each spear and cut the remainder of the stalks across in 5-mm / ¹/₄-inch rounds.

Remove the pastry case from the oven and discard the beans and paper. Return the pastry case to the oven to dry for 2 minutes.

Reduce the oven temperature to 180°C / 350°F / gas 4. Spread the onion over the bottom of the hot pastry case. Arrange the rounds of asparagus stalk on top. Crumble the cheese and scatter over the asparagus. Whisk the eggs and cream together and season with salt and pepper. Pour into the pastry case. Arrange the asparagus tips on top and press down into the egg mixture so they are just showing.

Bake the tart for 30–40 minutes or until golden brown and the filling is set. Serve warm or cold.

CHICKEN LIVERS AND HOT GOAT'S CHEESE WITH BABY SPINACH

Serves 4

TIP
For even more flavour, first marinate the goat's cheese in olive oil flavoured with garlic cloves and sprigs of fresh thyme and rosemary for at least 6 hours or overnight.

2 round Crottin de Chavignol or 4 slices
  of another firm goat's cheese, each 2-cm /
  3/4-inch thick
160 g / 5 1/2 oz chicken livers
4 large handfuls of baby spinach
4 slices of streaky bacon [US Canadian bacon]
1 tbsp sesame seeds
100 ml / 3 1/2 fl oz / 7 tbsp double cream
  [US heavy whipping cream]

2 tsp vegetable oil
strips of Dried Tomatoes (see page 17),
  to garnish (optional)

For the vinaigrette
4 1/2 tbsp olive oil
1 1/2 tbsp balsamic vinegar
1/2 tsp lemon juice
salt and freshly ground black pepper

If using Crottin de Chavignol, cut each one horizontally in half to make 2 discs.

Clean the chicken livers, removing all very dark or green bits. Cut into bite-size pieces. Remove any stalks from the spinach, then wash the leaves and dry them thoroughly. Remove any rind from the bacon. Mix together the vinaigrette ingredients in a small bowl.

Heat the grill [US broiler].

Heat a small frying pan over moderate heat. Add the sesame seeds and stir until they are lightly toasted. Set aside.

Put the cream in a small pan and boil to reduce to about 2 tbsp. Meanwhile, grill the bacon until it is crisp and browned. Cut it across into strips and keep warm.

Arrange the slices of goat's cheese on the grill pan and top each with 1/2 tbsp of the reduced cream. Grill for about 3 minutes or until the cheese is soft and lightly browned on top.

Heat the vegetable oil in a small frying pan over high heat and cook the chicken livers for 1 1/2–2 minutes or until they are browned but still pink inside, stirring and tossing constantly. Season with salt and pepper and keep warm.

Toss the spinach, sesame seeds and warm bacon in the vinaigrette. Spoon the chicken livers in a mound in the centre of each warmed plate and surround with the spinach mixture. Set the cheese on top of the chicken livers. Garnish with strips of dried tomatoes, if using, and serve immediately.

SWEETBREAD PURSES WITH TEMPURA VEGETABLES

Serves 4

200 g / 7 oz calf's sweetbreads
1/2 bay leaf
2 small onions
1 clove
1/2 garlic clove
15 g / 1/2 oz / 1 tbsp unsalted butter
1 tbsp vegetable oil plus more for deep frying
100 g / 3 1/2 oz button mushrooms

salt and freshly ground black pepper
3 1/2 tbsp double cream [US heavy whipping cream]
4 squares of filo pastry dough, each 17 x 17cm / 7 x 7 inches
1 egg yolk
4 squares of filo pastry dough, each 21 x 21cm / 8 1/2 x 8 1/2 inches
Tempura Vegetables (see page 148), to serve

Soak the sweetbreads in cold water for 2 hours, changing the water often. Drain, then rinse the sweetbreads under cold running water and peel off the excess skin and fat. Put them in a saucepan of salted water. Secure the bay leaf to one of the peeled onions with the clove and add to the pan. Bring to the boil, then simmer for about 20 minutes, skimming frequently. Remove from the heat and leave to cool.

Drain the sweetbreads. Cut off all the skin as well as any gristle, then cut into 5-mm / 1/4-inch dice. Set aside.

Peel and finely chop the remaining onion. Peel and chop the garlic to a paste (see page 13). Heat the butter and 1 tbsp oil in a frying pan and cook the onion until soft and translucent, stirring often. Add the garlic and cook for 1 minute longer.

Wash and dry the mushrooms and cut them in half. Add to the pan and season with salt and pepper. Cook over moderate heat, stirring constantly, for about 5 minutes. Stir in the cream and simmer until the liquid has reduced by half. Remove the mushrooms with a slotted spoon and cool, then chop finely. Meanwhile, boil the liquid in the pan until thick. Stir in the mushrooms and sweetbreads, and taste

and adjust the seasoning. Leave to cool completely.

Place one of the smaller squares of filo dough in a shallow dish that is about 6 cm / 2 1/2 inches in diameter (a ramekin or an oeuf en cocotte dish). Spoon one-quarter of the sweetbread mixture into the centre.

Lightly beat the egg yolk with 1 tsp water and brush this around the edges of the filo square. Bring the corners and sides of the square up over the filling and press together to seal to make a neat round parcel. Remove the parcel from the dish.

Put one of the larger squares of filo dough in the dish and brush all over with egg wash. Set the prepared filo parcel in the centre. Bring up all the points of the star around the parcel. Dab with a little egg wash and pinch them together at the top to seal well. Make 3 more filo purses in the same way.

Heat oil for deep frying to 160°C / 325°F.

Lower the filo purses into the hot oil and fry for about 3 minutes or until crisp and golden brown, turning so that they brown evenly. Drain on paper towels.

Arrange a filo purse and some tempura vegetables on each plate and garnish with parsley. Serve immediately.

RIGHT
Sweetbread Purses with Tempura Vegetables

TUNA TOASTS WITH ORANGE VINAIGRETTE

Serves 4

8 medium-thick slices of white bread
2 slices of tuna fillet, 1-cm / ¹/₂-inch thick,
    each weighing about 145 g / 5 oz
sea salt and freshly ground black pepper
2 egg yolks
2 whole eggs
2 tbsp freshly grated Parmesan cheese
1–2 tbsp vegetable oil
30 g / 1 oz / 2 tbsp unsalted butter

4 tbsp crème fraîche or sour cream
2 tbsp chopped fresh chives

For the orange vinaigrette
juice of 2 large oranges
2¹/₂ tsp sherry vinegar
1 tsp Dijon mustard
a pinch of sugar
100 ml / 3¹/₂ fl oz / 7 tbsp olive oil

TIPS

If you prefer, you can cut each sandwich into one or more rounds using pastry cutters [US cookie cutters] of varying size.

You could also use salmon for this dish.

First make the orange vinaigrette. Put the orange juice in a small pan and boil until reduced by three-quarters. Pour into a bowl and set aside to cool completely. Add the vinegar, mustard and sugar to the concentrated orange juice and whisk together until smooth. Slowly whisk in the oil. Season to taste with salt and pepper.

Trim the crusts from the bread. Roll over each slice of bread with a rolling pin to flatten it as much as possible. Cut each slice of tuna in half. If necessary, trim the tuna slices so they are about 5 mm / ¹/₄ inch smaller all around than the bread slices. Season the tuna with black pepper. Put a slice of tuna on 4 of the bread slices. Lightly beat the egg yolks with 1 tsp water. Brush this egg wash around the edge of each slice of bread, then cover with

a second slice of bread to form a sandwich. Press the edges together to seal. Trim the edges to neaten them.

Combine the whole eggs and Parmesan in a shallow dish and season with salt and pepper. Mix together with a fork.

Heat a large frying pan over moderately high heat, then add the oil and butter. Turn the tuna toasts in the egg mixture to coat on both sides, then add to the pan. Fry for about 1¹/₂ minutes on each side or until golden brown. The tuna will be rare in the centre.

Cut each tuna toast into 4 triangles and arrange on warmed plates. Quickly mix the cream and chives and put a spoonful on each plate. Whisk the vinaigrette briefly to emulsify it again and pour around the tuna toasts. Serve immediately.

ROASTED GARLIC WITH RYE BREAD AND BUTTER

Serves 4

TIP

Keep the chillies in a jar with the oil and use them in salads and pasta dishes.

4 heads of new season's garlic
4 fresh hot red chilli peppers
3 1/2 tbsp olive oil
unsalted butter

warmed peasant-style rye bread or other
coarse-textured brown bread
sea salt

Heat the oven to 180°C / 350°F / gas 4.

Cut each head of garlic across in half. Put the halves, cut side down, in a pan of boiling water and blanch for 1 minute. Drain and blanch again in fresh boiling water. Drain and leave to dry, cut side down, on a kitchen cloth.

Cut the chilli peppers lengthwise in half. Heat the oil in a roasting pan in the oven.

Put in the garlic, cut side down, and add the chillies. Roast for about 25 minutes. Remove from the oven and leave to cool in the oil. Put the chillies to one side.

Spread a little butter on slices of warmed bread. Press the garlic cloves out of their skin and spread on the bread. Mill a little sea salt over the top, and serve.

MARINATED FISH WITH ORANGE AND ROOT GINGER

Serves 4

You can use just one kind of fish, or scallops, or a mixture – say a slice each of salmon and brill and 2 slices of scallop for each serving. For the freshest flavour, the vegetables must be stir-fried and then served immediately. It's worth preparing twice the quantity suggested here because, if asked, everyone will want seconds.

*350 g / 12 oz very fresh skinless fish fillet
(salmon, brill or turbot) or large scallops
[US sea scallops] without roe (coral)*
sea salt and freshly ground black pepper
juice of 1 lemon
juice of 1 lime
2 medium-size chicory [US Belgian endive]
120 g / 4 oz small mange-tout [US snow peas]

60 g / 2 oz / 2/3 cup fresh beansprouts
1-cm / 1/2-inch piece of fresh root ginger
2 oranges
45 g / 1 1/2 oz / 1/2 cup pine nuts
1–2 tbsp groundnut oil [US peanut oil]
1 1/2 tsp sugar
*100 ml / 3 1/2 fl oz / 7 tbsp Soy and Balsamic
Vinaigrette (see page 21)*

Remove all bones from the fish fillet. With the knife at an angle, cut the fish fillet into very thin slices. If using scallops, cut them crosswise into thin slices. Lay the fish or scallop slices on a plate, in one layer, and season with salt and pepper. Sprinkle with the lemon and lime juices. Leave to marinate while you prepare the remaining ingredients, turning the slices over after 4–5 minutes.

Trim the core from the heads of chicory, then cut across into 1-cm / 1/2-inch strips. Trim the mange-tout, then cut them lengthwise in half. Rinse the beansprouts and pat dry with paper towels. Peel the ginger and chop it finely. Peel the oranges and remove the segments (see box). Toast the pine nuts (see page 84).

Heat a wok or heavy-based frying pan over moderately high heat. Add the oil and heat it, then stir-fry the mange-tout, beansprouts and ginger for 1 minute. Add the chicory and continue stir-frying for about 30 seconds or until the vegetables are just tender but still crunchy. Add the sugar and season with salt and pepper. Remove from the heat and stir in the orange segments.

Spoon the vegetable mixture on to warmed plates. Drain the marinated fish and arrange on top of the vegetables in loose folds like fabric. Spoon over the vinaigrette and sprinkle with the toasted pine nuts. Serve immediately.

TO SEGMENT AN ORANGE
Peel it, removing all the white pith. Holding it over a bowl to catch the juice, cut on both sides of each dividing membrane to remove the segments. As each segment is removed, fold back the membrane like the pages of a book.

MARINATED VEGETABLE SALAD WITH STAR ANISE

Serves 6-8

This is very nice as a first course in the summer, or it could be served as a cold vegetable.

2 globe artichokes
1/2 lemon
2 small fennel bulbs
120 g / 4 oz courgettes [US zucchini]
120 g / 4 oz small tender carrots
60 g / 2 oz button onions [US pearl onions]
120 g / 4 oz small button mushrooms
120 g / 4 oz ripe but firm plum tomatoes
4 tbsp olive oil

120 g / 4 oz cauliflower florets
3 tbsp dry white wine
3 tbsp white wine vinegar
about 450 ml / 3/4 pint / nearly 2 cups
  Chicken Essence (see page 14)
2 star anise
1 bay leaf
1 tsp black peppercorns
salt and freshly ground black pepper

Break the stalk from each artichoke. Pull off the large outside leaves, then cut off all the smaller leaves. When you reach the hairy choke, scoop it out. Trim any remaining leaf or stalk from the artichoke bottom. Cut each artichoke bottom into quarters. Rub all over with the lemon half to prevent the artichokes discolouring.

Trim the fennel bulbs, then cut each one lengthwise into quarters.

Trim the courgettes and cut across into 5-mm / 1/4-inch slices. Peel the carrots and cut across into 5-mm / 1/4-inch slices.

Peel the onions. Trim off the mushroom stalks. Peel the tomatoes and remove the seeds (see page 74), then cut the tomato flesh into 1-cm / 1/2-inch dice.

Heat the oil in a flameproof casserole over low heat and add the artichokes, fennel, carrots, onions and cauliflower florets. Stir to coat the vegetables with oil. Cook for 3 minutes, stirring occasionally. Add the mushrooms and cook for 2 minutes

longer, then add the courgettes and cook for a further 30 seconds.

Heat the oven to 180°C / 350°F / gas 4.

Stir in the wine and vinegar and bring to the boil. Simmer, uncovered, until the liquid has reduced to a glaze, stirring constantly.

Pour enough chicken essence into the casserole just to cover the vegetables. Add the star anise and bay leaf. Crush the peppercorns coarsely with the base of a heavy pan and add to the vegetables.

Cover the casserole and transfer it to the oven. Cook for 12–15 minutes or until the vegetables are tender but still firm.

Remove from the oven. After 5 minutes, stir in the tomatoes, then leave to cool completely.

Season with salt and pepper. Serve the vegetables at room temperature, with a spoonful or two of the liquid spooned over them.

TOMATO AND MOZZARELLA TARTS

Serves 4

Make the tarts when plum tomatoes are in season and full of the flavour of sun-ripened fruit.

300 g / 10 oz *Puff Pastry (see page 27)*
4 ripe but firm plum tomatoes
300 g / 10 oz mozzarella cheese, preferably buffalo mozzarella

truffle oil (optional)
salt and freshly ground black pepper
4 tbsp Pesto Sauce (see page 24)
sprigs of fresh basil, to garnish

Roll out the puff pastry to 3 mm / ⅛ inch thickness. Cut out 4 discs, each 15 cm / 6 inches in diameter. Transfer the discs to a large baking sheet and chill for 1 hour.

Heat the oven to 200°C / 400°F / gas 6.

Prick the pastry discs all over with a fork. Bake for 6 minutes or until they are lightly browned and crisp. Turn them over and bake for a further 4 minutes. Allow to cool on a wire rack.

Peel the tomatoes (see box), then cut them into 5-mm / ¼-inch slices. Cut the mozzarella cheeses in half, then cut them into slices the same thickness as the tomato slices.

Just before serving, preheat the oven to 200°C / 400°F / gas 6. Brush the pastry discs with a little truffle oil, if using.

Arrange the slices of tomato and mozzarella on the pastry discs, alternating tomato and mozzarella and overlapping the slices slightly. Season generously with salt and pepper, and spoon the pesto sauce on top of each tart. Bake for about 5 minutes or until heated through and the mozzarella has softened.

Sprinkle lightly with truffle oil and give a turn with the pepper mill. Garnish with basil sprigs and serve.

TO PEEL AND SEED TOMATOES

TO PEEL TOMATOES, cut a criss-cross in the skin on the base of each tomato and cut out the stalk. Put the tomatoes in a wire basket and immerse in a pan of boiling water for 10 seconds. Lift out the basket and immerse it in a bowl of iced water. Drain the tomatoes. Their skins will peel off easily.

TO SEED TOMATOES, cut the tomatoes into quarters and scrape out the seeds with a knife or teaspoon.

TIPS

Truffle oil is extra virgin olive oil flavoured with truffles. It is very intense in flavour, and can be used in pasta sauces, potato purée, and, in tiny quantities, in salads. A little truffle oil enhances the flavour of tomatoes; however, be sparing because too much will overpower the dish.

Always use plum tomatoes because they are firmer than other tomatoes.

Don't arrange the tomato and mozzarella slices on the pastry discs until the last moment, otherwise the pastry could become soggy with juice from the tomatoes.

The puff pastry you can buy these days from supermarkets is excellent and saves you hours of work.

RIGHT
Tomato and Mozzarella Tart

LANGOUSTINE
CEVICHE

Serves 4

4 large live langoustines or Dublin Bay prawns,
  each weighing 75–90 g / 2¹/₂–3 oz
2 shallots or ¹/₂ small onion
¹/₂ small garlic clove
1 ripe but firm plum tomato
4 sprigs of fresh basil
2 tbsp olive oil
1¹/₂ tbsp brandy
100 ml / 3¹/₂ fl oz / 7 tbsp dry white wine
100 ml / 3¹/₂ fl oz / 7 tbsp Chicken Essence
  (see page 14)

1¹/₂ tbsp double cream [US heavy whipping
  cream]
100 g / 3¹/₂ oz / 7 tbsp cold unsalted butter
salt and freshly ground white pepper
cayenne pepper
1 tbsp fresh lime juice
2 tsp fresh lemon juice
2 tbsp cooked green peas, preferably fresh
4 large fresh dill sprigs, to garnish

TIPS

Should the sauce
separate, heat a
spoonful of cream in a
separate pan, remove
from the heat and
whisk in 30 g / 1 oz /
2 tbsp of the butter.
Add this to the sauce,
spoonful by spoonful.

Freezing the lan-
goustines enables
them to be cut into
the thinnest possible
slices. They will thaw
in seconds.

Bring a pan of salted water to the boil. Put the langoustines in a wire basket, immerse them in the boiling water and then lift out immediately. Refresh in iced water and drain well.

Pull off the heads. With scissors, snip open the shell on the curved underside of each langoustine. Peel off the shells. Set the heads and shells aside. Dry the langoustines well, then lay each one flat on a piece of freezer film. Wrap and freeze while making the sauce.

Peel and finely chop the shallots or onion. Peel the garlic and chop to a paste (see page 13). Chop the tomato. Pull the basil stalks from the leaves and set the leaves aside.

Heat the oil in a saucepan over low heat and cook the shallots until soft and translucent, stirring often. Add the garlic and cook for 1 minute longer.

Crush the langoustine heads and shells with a rolling pin. Add to the pan with the tomato and basil stalks. Cook over high heat for 2–3 minutes, stirring frequently.

Add the brandy and let it warm slightly, then set it alight. When the flames die down, stir in the wine and chicken essence and bring to the boil. Boil for about 8 minutes or until reduced by two-thirds. Add the cream and boil until reduced by half.

Cut the butter into small pieces and add them a few at a time to the sauce, swirling it in the pan to melt and mix in the butter. Press the sauce through a fine sieve into a clean saucepan. Season with salt and cayenne pepper. Keep the sauce warm.

Brush each plate with a little lime and lemon juice and sprinkle with salt and pepper. Cut each langoustine into very thin slices, preferably no thicker than 1 mm / less than ¹/₁₆ inch, and arrange on the plates in a single layer, in a ring. Season with pepper and brush lightly with lime and lemon juice.

Cut the basil leaves into fine strips. Add to the sauce with the peas and a squeeze of lime juice. Pour a fine ring of sauce around the langoustines and garnish with a dill sprig in the centre of each plate.

SLICES OF BEEF FILLET WITH SPINACH AND PARMESAN

Serves 4

200 g / 7 oz beef fillet [US beef tenderloin]
a small handful of baby spinach leaves
juice of 1/2 lemon
1 1/2 tsp extra virgin olive oil

1 1/2 tsp truffle oil or additional olive oil
salt and freshly ground black pepper
40-g / 1 2/3-oz piece of Parmesan cheese

Remove all fat and skin from the beef. Chill the beef in the freezer for about 20 minutes to firm it up.

Meanwhile, remove any stalks from the spinach, then wash the leaves and dry thoroughly.

Cut the beef across the grain into wafer-thin slices. Put the slices between sheets of cling film [US plastic wrap] and pound gently with a mallet or meat pounder to flatten slightly. Do not break the fibres in the meat or make any holes.

Mix together the lemon juice and oils.

Brush a little of the mixture over 4 large plates and season with salt and pepper. Arrange the slices of beef on the plates in one layer, slightly overlapping them if necessary. Brush the beef with the remaining lemon and oil mixture and season with salt and pepper.

Toss the spinach leaves in a little of the oil mixture, season and arrange on the centre of each plate of beef. Cut paper-thin shavings of Parmesan using a swivel-bladed vegetable peeler and scatter over the beef and spinach. Serve immediately.

POTATO SALAD WITH CAVIAR
À LA RAISA

Serves 4

The warm potatoes and slight acidity of the crème fraîche together with the caviar make a spectacular dish. This was created for Mrs Gorbachev when she visited London.

600 g / 1 1/4 lb small new potatoes
100 ml / 3 1/2 fl oz / 7 tbsp crème fraîche or
    sour cream
2 tbsp Mayonnaise (see page 24)
2 tbsp chopped fresh chives

salt and freshly ground black pepper
50 g / 3/4 oz caviar, preferably Ocietra or
    Sevruga
4 small handfuls of lamb's lettuce (mâche)
2 tsp Sherry Vinaigrette (see page 21)

Wash the potatoes, then put them in a pan of salted water. Bring to the boil and cook for 10–15 minutes or until the potatoes are just tender. Drain. When the potatoes are cool enough to handle, peel them. Cut into 5-mm / 1/4-inch slices and keep warm.

Combine the crème fraîche, mayonnaise and chives in a bowl. Season with pepper and mix well. Add the potatoes and fold in to dress each slice. Add three-quarters of the caviar and mix very gently with the potatoes, lifting the slices so as not to break the caviar.

Spoon the potato and caviar salad into the centre of the plates and top with the remaining caviar. Toss the lamb's lettuce in the vinaigrette, then arrange around the potato and caviar salad. Serve immediately.

RIGHT
*Potato Salad with
Caviar à la Raisa*

GAME PÂTÉ

Serves 12

You can use any kind of game meat to make this hearty pâté – from other game animals or game birds. If you use a game bird and also have boneless breast pieces, fry these quickly in a little hot oil just to brown them (the inside should still be rare), then lay the breasts in a layer in the centre of the mixture in the terrine.

200 g / 7 oz belly of pork [US fresh pork side]
200 g / 7 oz boneless hare or venison
200 g / 7 oz boneless lean pork, preferably loin
200 g / 7 oz pork back fat [US pork fatback]
200 g / 7 oz hare or game bones
2 tbsp vegetable oil
2 garlic cloves
2 onions
15 g / 1/2 oz / 1 tbsp unsalted butter
1 sprig of fresh thyme
6 juniper berries
4 black peppercorns
3 tbsp brandy
finely grated zest and juice of 1 unwaxed orange
200 ml / 7 fl oz / 7/8 cup port wine
500 ml / 16 fl oz / 2 cups Chicken Concentrate
  (see page 16)

30 g / 1 oz / 1/4 cup shelled pistachio nuts
1 egg
1 egg yolk
250 ml / 8 fl oz / 1 cup double cream
  [US heavy whipping cream]
salt and freshly ground black pepper
finely grated zest of 1 unwaxed lemon
300 g / 10 oz (about 10 slices) smoked
  streaky bacon [US Canadian bacon] or
  slices of pork back fat
3 bay leaves

For the garnish
a handful of curly endive for each plate
Sherry Vinaigrette (see page 21)
a few walnut halves

Remove any tough skin from the belly of pork. Cut the hare or venison, pork, pork belly and pork fat into cubes. Pass the cubes of meat and fat through the medium plate / disc of a mincer [US meat grinder]. You can also use a food processor, but work one type of meat at a time and do not reduce the meats to a paste.

Heat the oven to 220°C / 425°F / gas 7.

Chop the hare bones (or ask your butcher to do this for you). Heat a small roasting pan on top of the stove, then add half of the oil and put in the bones. Transfer to the oven and roast for about 10 minutes or until the bones are browned.

Peel the garlic and chop it to a paste (see page 13).

Peel and chop the onions. Heat the remaining oil and the butter in a saucepan over low heat and cook half of the onions until soft, stirring often. Add half of the garlic and the thyme and cook gently for 1 minute longer. Allow to cool, then remove and discard the thyme stalks. Add the onion mixture to the minced meats.

Add the remaining onion and garlic to the bones and stir well. Roast for a further 5 minutes.

Lightly crush the juniper berries and peppercorns with the base of a heavy pan.

Set the roasting pan over moderate heat on top of the stove. Add the brandy and heat it, then set it alight. When the flames have died down, add the orange juice and port and stir very well. Bring to the boil and boil until reduced by half. Stir in the chicken concentrate and crushed juniper berries and peppercorns and boil until reduced by two-thirds. Strain the glaze and allow to cool.

Skin the pistachios (see page 24). Chop the nuts coarsely.

Combine the minced meats, cold glaze, egg and egg yolk and work well together. Slowly mix in the cream. Season well with salt and pepper. Mix in the pistachio nuts and orange and lemon zests.

Heat the oven to 150°C / 300°F / gas 2.

Use the bacon slices to line a 1.2-litre / 2-pint / 5-cup terrine mould, laying the slices across the mould and leaving them hanging over the rim. Fill the mould with the meat mixture, pressing it down well. Fold the ends of the bacon slices over the surface and arrange the bay leaves on top. Bang the mould lightly on a damp cloth to settle the contents.

Cover the mould with a lid or foil and set it in a roasting pan containing enough hot water to come halfway up the sides of the mould. Place in the oven and cook for about 1 hour 5 minutes. To test if the pâté is cooked, insert a skewer in the centre and press the top of the pâté; the juices that rise should not be pink. Allow the pâté to cool completely. Cover and refrigerate it for at least 6 hours.

To unmould the pâté, loosen it all around with a knife, then turn it upside down on a board and bang the base of the mould firmly. Lift off the mould, and turn the pâté over right side up.

Serve the pâté at cool room temperature, cut into finger-thick slices. Garnish each plate with a handful of curly endive tossed in vinaigrette. Top the endive with a few walnut halves. Serve with Cumberland sauce (see box) and good country-style bread.

CUMBERLAND SAUCE

Pare the zest from 2 unwaxed oranges and 1 unwaxed lemon, without taking any of the white pith. Cut the zest into very fine strips. Caramelize the strips (see page 160). Squeeze the juice from the oranges and lemon and combine in a saucepan with 400 ml / 14 fl oz / 1 3/4 cups port wine, 200 ml / 7 fl oz / 7/8 cup Chicken Essence (see page 16) and 200 g / 7 oz / 2/3 cup redcurrant jelly. Peel and chop 1 shallot. Lightly crush 12 black peppercorns with the base of a heavy pan. Add the shallot and peppercorns to the pan with a pinch of ground ginger. Bring to the boil and simmer for 10 minutes or until the sauce starts to thicken slightly. Strain the sauce through a fine sieve. Stir in a small piece of unsalted butter and the caramelized strips of zest and allow to cool.

MARINATED HERRING AND POTATO TERRINE WITH APPLE AND CHIVE CREAM SAUCE

Serves 8-10

2 large, long leeks, white and pale green parts only
200 g / 7 oz large carrots
150 g / 5 oz large potato
150 g / 5 oz French beans [US thin greenbeans]
225 g / 8 oz ripe but firm plum tomatoes
salt and freshly ground black pepper
450 g / 1 lb marinated herrings with onions, preferably Matjes herrings, half spiced and half with dill

120 g / 4 oz / 8 tbsp [1 stick] unsalted butter

For the apple and chive cream sauce
1/2 apple
100 ml / 3 1/2 fl oz / 7 tbsp crème fraîche or sour cream
2 tbsp Mayonnaise (see page 22)
1 tbsp lemon juice
2 tbsp chopped fresh chives

Trim the leeks, slit them open lengthwise and wash thoroughly. Cook in boiling salted water until tender, then drain and refresh in iced water. Drain again and set aside.

Peel the carrots and cut across into 7.5-cm / 3-inch pieces. Cook in boiling salted water until tender, then drain. Refresh in iced water and drain again. When cool enough to handle, cut the pieces of carrot lengthwise into 5-mm / 1/4-inch sticks. Set aside.

Cook the potato in boiling salted water until tender, then drain. Peel the potato and cut it into 5-mm / 1/4-inch sticks. Set aside.

Trim the beans and blanch them in boiling salted water until just tender. Drain and refresh in iced water, then drain again and set aside.

Peel the tomatoes, cut them into quarters and remove the seeds (see page 74). Season the carrots, potato, beans and tomatoes with salt and pepper.

Drain the herrings and reserve the marinated onions. Pat both herrings and onions dry with paper towels. Cut the herrings lengthwise into strips.

Peel apart the leek leaves and dry them well with paper towels. Season them with salt and pepper. Line a 1-litre / 2-pint / 1-quart capacity terrine mould with cling film [US plastic wrap]. Lay the leek leaves in the mould crosswise to line the bottom and sides evenly, leaving about 3 cm / 1 1/4 inches hanging over the sides.

Melt the butter. Make alternate layers of the prepared vegetables, strips of herring and marinated onions in the mould, dipping the vegetables in melted butter before putting them in the mould. When the mould is full, fold the ends of the leek leaves over the top. Cover with cling film and put a weight on the top. Refrigerate for at least 4 hours.

Meanwhile, make the sauce. Peel and core the apple and cut into very fine dice. Combine the apple with the remaining ingredients and mix well. Cover and chill until ready to serve.

Remove the mould from the refrigerator and turn out the terrine. Peel off the cling film, then cut the terrine across into 1.5-cm / 3/4-inch slices.

Place a slice of terrine in the centre of each plate and add a spoonful of the sauce. Serve with hot buttered toast.

TIPS
The terrine will keep well for 2–3 days in the refrigerator.

Other vegetables such as baby leeks, asparagus and broccoli can be used instead of those suggested here. You could also substitute fried sole fillets or scallops for the marinated herring.

WINTER SALAD OF PRESERVED DUCK WITH BEETROOT

Serves 4

4 medium-sized beetroot [US beets]
2 tbsp white wine vinegar
2 tbsp olive oil
1 1/2 tsp sugar
salt and freshly ground black pepper
4 handfuls of curly endive
4 tbsp Sherry Vinaigrette (see page 21)
Croûtons (see page 51), to finish

For the preserved duck
4 duck leg portions
30 g / 1 oz / 3 1/2 tbsp sea salt
3 shallots
2 garlic cloves
5 sprigs of fresh thyme
100 ml / 3 1/2 fl oz / 7 tbsp tarragon vinegar
200 g / 7 oz goose fat

First prepare the preserved duck. Remove all excess fat from the duck legs. Cut the joint between the thigh and drumstick without separating them. Rub the sea salt well into the legs. Put the legs in a bowl.

Peel and chop the shallots. Peel the garlic and roughly crush with the side of a knife. Add the shallots and garlic to the bowl together with the thyme and tarragon vinegar. Season with pepper. Add the goose fat and mix well with your fingers so that the duck legs are evenly coated with the fat and seasonings. Cover and set aside in a cool place to marinate for at least 12 hours or overnight.

Heat the oven to 120°C / 250°F / gas 1/4.

Scrape the marinade from the duck legs and place them in a roasting pan. Transfer the marinade to a small pan and heat it gently until melted. Pour it over the duck legs; they should be well covered. Cook in the oven for 6–7 hours or until the meat is falling off the bone. The fat must not bubble, so reduce the temperature slightly if necessary.

Remove from the oven and leave to cool completely. (You can now pack the preserved duck and its cooking liquid into a tightly covered container and store in the refrigerator until needed.)

Put the beetroot in a pan of salted water and bring to the boil. Simmer until tender. Drain and when cool enough to handle, peel the beetroot. Cut each one in half, then cut the halves across into 5-mm / 1/4-inch slices.

Mix together the white wine vinegar, olive oil, sugar and 1 tbsp of water in a bowl. Add the beetroot slices and season with salt and pepper. Stir gently, then set aside to marinate for 15 minutes.

Meanwhile, scrape all the fat from the preserved duck legs. Take off the skin, cut it into strips and reserve it. Remove all the meat from the bones and cut into 1-cm / 1/2-inch cubes. Wash the endive and dry.

Heat the grill [US broiler]. Put the strips of duck skin on a baking sheet and grill until they are crisp, stirring so they brown evenly. Drain on paper towels.

Toss the cubes of duck and the endive with the vinaigrette. Season.

Drain the beetroot and divide among the plates. Pile the duck and endive mixture on top. Sprinkle croûtons around the salad and sprinkle the crisp duck skin on top.

SALAD OF LOBSTER IN A CURRY DRESSING

Serves 4

With the availability of Canadian lobster, the price has come down over the last few years, so lobster need not be thought of as an unaffordable luxury.

Vegetable Essence (see page 12)
4 live lobsters, each weighing about 450 g / 1 lb
45 g / 1 1/2 oz / 1/2 cup pine nuts
1 small crisp apple
4 small handfuls of mixed curly endive and sliced radicchio leaves, weighing about 90 g / 3 oz

salt and freshly ground white pepper
2 tbsp Sherry Vinaigrette (see page 21)
120 ml / 4 fl oz / 1/2 cup Curry Dressing (see page 22)
2 tbsp chopped fresh chives

Bring a large pot of vegetable essence or salted water to the boil. Put the lobsters in the pot and boil for 8 minutes. Remove the lobsters and put them in a bowl of iced water for 5 minutes. Drain and set aside to cool completely.

Toast the pine nuts (see box).

When the lobsters are cool, break off the claws and head; discard the head. Using poultry shears or a heavy, sharp knife, crack the claws and remove the meat in one piece. Hold each lobster tail shell side down and, with poultry shears or strong scissors, split it open lengthwise. Remove the piece of lobster tail meat from the shell. Cut each lobster tail lengthwise into 4 pieces.

Peel the apple, cut it into quarters and remove the core. Cut each quarter lengthwise into 4 thin slices.

Arrange the pieces of lobster tail meat in the centre of 4 plates with a slice of apple between each slice of lobster. Place the 2 shelled lobster claws on either side.

Mix the toasted pine nuts with the curly endive and radicchio. Season to taste with salt and pepper and toss with the vinaigrette. Put a small pile at the top of each plate.

Grind some pepper over the lobster and spoon over a little of the curry dressing. Sprinkle with the chives and serve.

TIPS

If you have some vegetable essence, cook the lobsters in it because it will give the lobster meat more flavour.

Be sure not to over-cook lobster or the meat will become dry and stringy.

When preparing lobster to be served cold, it is best to cook it 24 hours in advance and then to refrigerate it before removing the shell.

If you are assembling the salad in advance of serving, sprinkle the apple slices with a little lemon juice to prevent them discolouring.

TO TOAST NUTS

Spread the nuts in a shallow pan and toast under the grill [US broiler] until golden brown, shaking the pan occasionally to turn the nuts and brown all sides.

MAIN COURSES

THE main dish is the central focus of any meal. When planning a menu, it should be decided upon first and then, depending on the colour, balance, taste and texture of the main dish, the first and following courses can be chosen. These other courses should not repeat the characteristics of the main course.

Here I have grouped fish, poultry, game and meat main dishes. A number of the fish dishes could also be served as first courses, if you reduce the quantities. Each recipe gives the cooking method suitable for the type and cut of fish, fowl or meat.

It is essential that the grill or oven be heated to the temperature specified in the recipe and that the timing suggested be followed; this is particularly important when cooking fish, to ensure that it is not dried out, thus ruining the taste and texture.

Good quality ingredients are vital for success. I always use wild rather than farmed fish and game, properly hung and butchered meat, free-range chickens, and fresh plump brains and sweetbreads. The fresher fish is, the better, so try to use local fish and shellfish.

Offal divides the nation – there are those who believe it is the food of the gods and those who believe it is pure hell! Unless you know your friends are offal fans it is not a good thing to serve at dinner parties. I find the taste, texture and colour of calf's liver, kidneys, sweetbreads and brains to be irresistible, but I am afraid that others don't.

FISH STEW WITH SAFFRON AND FENNEL

Serves 4

Fish with fennel – a marriage made in heaven.

45 g / 1¹/₂ oz vermicelli
100 g / 3¹/₂ oz Chinese leaves [US Napa
* cabbage]*
¹/₂ red sweet pepper
¹/₂ green sweet pepper
700 g / 1¹/₂ lb mixed fish fillets, preferably
* 225 g / 8 oz each of 3 types, such as red*
* mullet, skate, salmon, bream, sea bass,*
* hake, haddock, turbot, pike*

sea salt and freshly ground black pepper
4 tbsp olive oil
a pinch of saffron
1 litre / 1³/₄ pints / 1 quart Chicken Essence
* (see page 14)*
100 g / 3¹/₂ oz / ²/₃ cup sweetcorn kernels
* [US whole kernel corn], fresh, canned or*
* thawed frozen*
1 tbsp chopped fresh herb fennel

Cook the vermicelli in boiling salted water until it is just tender to the bite. Drain it well and refresh under cold running water. Set aside.

Shred the Chinese leaves into very fine strips. Using a vegetable peeler, peel the sweet peppers, then remove the seeds and cut the flesh into fine strips.

Heat the grill [US broiler] and the grill pan with rack in place.

Cut each of the 3 types of fish into 4 pieces. Season with salt and pepper, then turn them in the olive oil to coat.

Put the saffron and chicken essence in a saucepan and bring to a simmer. Add the sweet peppers and sweetcorn and simmer for 3 minutes. (If using fresh sweetcorn, it will need 6 minutes' cooking.) Add the Chinese leaves and cook for a further 1 minute.

Meanwhile, arrange the fish on the hot grill rack and grill until it is just cooked and opaque. Test with the point of a knife: the flesh in the centre should still be slightly translucent.

Add the vermicelli and fennel to the vegetables and stir to mix. Taste and adjust the seasoning. Ladle into warmed soup plates. Arrange the fish in the centre, giving each serving one piece of each type of fish. Give the fish a turn of the peppermill, and serve.

TIPS

If you prefer, cut the fish into bite-size strips and stir them into the soup for serving.

You could also poach the fish in the soup, instead of grilling it.

RIGHT
Fish Stew with Saffron
and Fennel

TOADSTOOLS OF SOLE WITH A SPICY VEGETABLE SAUCE

Serves 4

1 small onion
45 g / 1¹/₂ oz / 3 tbsp unsalted butter
150 g / 5 oz button mushrooms
sea salt and freshly ground black pepper
6 tbsp double cream [US heavy whipping cream]
1 green sweet pepper

1 red sweet pepper
skinned fillets from 4 Dover sole
16 large fresh basil leaves
8 Pastry Discs (see page 27)
300 ml / ¹/₂ pint / 1¹/₄ cups Spicy Vegetable Sauce (see page 20)

TIPS
The spicy vegetable sauce can be made ahead of time and then reheated while you are steaming the sole rolls.

If you prefer, just lay the sole rolls in the centre of the plates, spoon the sauce over and around them, and set the pastry discs on the edge of the plate.

Peel and finely chop the onion. Heat 30 g / 1 oz / 2 tbsp of the butter in a frying pan over low heat and cook the onion until soft and translucent, stirring often. Cut the mushrooms in half. Add to the pan and season with salt and pepper. Cook over a moderate heat, stirring constantly, for about 5 minutes. Stir in the cream and simmer until the liquid has reduced by half. Remove the mushrooms with a slotted spoon and cool, then chop finely. Meanwhile, boil the liquid in the pan until thick. Leave to cool completely, then stir in the mushrooms. Taste and adjust seasoning.

Peel the green and red peppers with a swivel-bladed vegetable peeler, then remove the core, seeds and white ribs. Very finely dice the flesh. Blanch the pepper dice in boiling salted water for 2 minutes. Drain and refresh in iced water. Drain again and set aside.

Make little criss-cross incisions down the skinned side of each sole fillet to prevent it curling during cooking. Place each fillet between 2 sheets of cling film [US plastic wrap] and pound lightly with the base of a heavy pan to flatten the fillet to about double its width.

Season the scored side of the sole fillets

with salt and pepper and put 2 basil leaves on each one. Divide the mushroom mixture among the fish and spread it over three-quarters of the fillet, starting from the thick end. Roll up each fillet from the thick end and secure with a skewer or wooden cocktail stick.

Bring water to the boil in a steamer. Arrange the sole rolls on the rack over the boiling water. Cover and steam for about 6 minutes or until the fish is opaque.

Meanwhile, reheat the pastry discs in the oven. Heat the remaining butter in a small pan and toss the pepper dice to reheat. Season with salt and pepper. Arrange the pepper dice in a ring on the warmed plates, leaving a 15-cm / 6-inch diameter round in the centre. Remove the skewers or sticks from the sole rolls. If necessary, trim one end to make a flat base, then set 2 sole rolls upright in the centre of each plate. Give the fish a turn of the peppermill.

Spoon the vegetable sauce over and around the sole rolls so that it fills in the space between them and the pepper ring. Top each sole roll with a pastry disc, one with poppy seeds and one with sesame seeds for each plate. Serve immediately.

FILLET OF SOLE IN RED PEPPER JUICE WITH LINGUINE

Serves 4

The red pepper juice has a unique, very intense flavour that requires no seasoning to enhance it. A vegetable juicer is needed. You can use any flat fish for this dish.

1 large fennel bulb, with feathery leaves
5 tbsp olive oil
4 red sweet peppers, weighing about 500 g / 1 lb 2 oz
sea salt and freshly ground black pepper

225 g / 8 oz fresh linguine (see tip)
fillets from 4 Dover sole, each fillet weighing about 90 g / 3 oz
2 tbsp freshly grated Parmesan cheese

Pull the feathery leaves from the fennel and set them aside. Trim the fennel bulb and cut it into very fine shreds. Heat 1½ tbsp of the oil in a small frying pan over low heat and cook the fennel gently, covered, until tender but still firm.

Meanwhile, cut the peppers in half and remove the stalks and seeds. Press the peppers in a vegetable juicer; you should obtain about 300 ml / ½ pint / 1¼ cups juice. Put the juice in a saucepan.

Heat the grill [US broiler] and the grill pan with rack in place. Bring a large pan of salted water to the boil.

Bring the pepper juice to the boil and boil until reduced to about 4 tbsp and slightly thickened.

Cook the linguine in the boiling water for 2–3 minutes or until just tender to the bite (*al dente*).

Season the sole fillets, turn them in 1–2 tbsp of the oil to coat and then place on the hot grill rack. Grill for about 3 minutes or until just cooked. Test with the point of a knife: the flesh in the centre should still be slightly translucent.

Drain the linguine and toss with the remaining olive oil. Add the fennel, feathery fennel tops and Parmesan. Season with salt and pepper.

Pile the pasta on warmed plates and arrange the sole fillets next to it. Pour the reduced red pepper juice around, give the fish a turn of the peppermill and serve immediately.

BRILL WITH ASPARAGUS AND TOMATO AND HERB DRESSING

Serves 4

This simple yet piquant summer dish is served lukewarm.

16 small asparagus spears
4 pieces of skinless brill fillet or fillets of other
  flat fish, each weighing about 140 g / 5 oz
sea salt and freshly ground black pepper
2 tbsp vegetable oil

a little unsalted butter
200 ml / 7 fl oz / 7/8 cup Plum Tomato and
  Herb Vinaigrette (see page 21)
4 tsp balsamic vinegar

Prepare the asparagus (see box). Cook it in boiling salted water until it is just tender but still firm. Drain well, then refresh in iced water.

Heat the oven to 200°C / 400°F / gas 6. Heat a ridged cast-iron grill pan until it is very hot.

Season the pieces of fish with salt and pepper, then turn in the oil to coat. Set the pieces of fish on the grill pan and rotate them to mark a criss-cross pattern, about 25 seconds on each side. Transfer the fish to a shallow pan or baking sheet and cover with buttered paper. Finish cooking in the oven for about 8 minutes or until the fish is opaque. Test with the point of a knife: the

flesh in the centre should still be slightly translucent.

Meanwhile, put the asparagus in a pan with a little butter and 1 tbsp water and heat until the water has evaporated and the asparagus is hot. Season with salt and pepper. Gently heat the tomato and herb vinaigrette (without the tomato dice and herbs) until it is lukewarm, then stir in the tomato and herbs.

Place the fish on warmed plates and give it a turn of the peppermill. Pour around the tomato and herb vinaigrette. Arrange the asparagus around the fish and sprinkle everything with the balsamic vinegar. Serve immediately.

TIP
Alternatively, you can cook the fish under a preheated grill [US broiler] for 5–6 minutes, turning once.

TO PREPARE ASPARAGUS

When in season, tender young asparagus spears need only have the 'leaves' on the sides of the stalks removed with a knife or vegetable peeler. If the ends of the stalks are woody, however, trim off the ends, then lay each spear on a chopping board and scrape the skin off the whole length of the stalk, working away from the tip.

RIGHT
Brill with Asparagus and Tomato and Herb Dressing

HAKE STEAK ON BUTTERED BEANS WITH PISTACHIO SAUCE

Serves 4

*200 g / 7 oz / 1 heaping cup dried butter
 beans [US dried Fordhook lima beans]*
1 onion
2 garlic cloves
1/2 bunch of watercress
45 g / 1 1/2 oz / 1/3 cup shelled pistachio nuts
6 tbsp groundnut oil [US peanut oil]

60 g / 2 oz / 4 tbsp unsalted butter
*800 ml / 1 1/3 pints / 3 1/4 cups Chicken
 Essence (see page 14)*
sea salt and freshly ground black pepper
*4, 8 or 12 hake steaks, 2.5-cm / 1-inch thick,
 weighing about 700 g / 1 1/2 lb*
flour for coating

Wash the beans thoroughly, then cook them in boiling water for 8 minutes. Drain and refresh under cold running water. Squeeze the beans gently in your fingers to slip off the skins.

Peel and finely chop the onion. Peel the garlic and chop to a paste (see page 13). Pull the watercress leaves from the stalks and set them aside; reserve the stalks. Skin the pistachio nuts (see page 24) and chop them.

Heat 1 tbsp of the oil with 15 g / 1/2 oz / 1 tbsp of the butter in a saucepan over a low heat and cook half of the onion until soft and translucent, stirring often. Add half of the garlic and cook gently for 1 minute longer. Stir in the beans and 500 ml / 16 fl oz / 2 cups of the chicken essence and bring to the boil. Simmer for about 30 minutes or until the beans are tender but still firm and the essence has evaporated.

Meanwhile, heat 1 tbsp oil with 15 g / 1/2 oz / 1 tbsp butter in another saucepan over low heat and soften the remaining onion. Add the remaining garlic and cook gently for 1 minute longer. Add the pistachios, watercress stalks and the remaining chicken essence. Season with salt and

pepper. Bring to the boil, then reduce the heat and simmer for about 15 minutes or until the pistachios have softened.

Remove and discard the watercress stalks. Add the watercress leaves and cook for a further 2 minutes.

Allow the sauce to cool slightly, then purée it in a blender or food processor. Pour it into a clean saucepan and set aside.

Season the hake steaks with salt and pepper and turn them in a little flour to coat lightly. Heat a large frying pan over moderate heat; add the remaining oil and then 10 g / 1/3 oz / 2 tsp butter. Fry the hake steaks, turning once, for about 5 minutes or until just cooked. When you turn them, add another 10 g / 1/3 oz / 2 tsp butter to the pan. Test the fish with the point of a knife: the flesh in the centre should still be slightly translucent.

Meanwhile, add the remaining butter to the beans and toss until the beans are coated. Season with salt and pepper. Reheat the sauce, and taste and adjust the seasoning.

Spoon the buttered beans on warmed plates and top with the hake steaks. Pour the sauce around and serve.

TIPS

The pistachio sauce can also be made with vegetable essence (see recipe on page 12), and used with vegetable dishes.

Hake can vary considerably in size. For this dish, each portion of fish should weigh about 175 g / 6 oz, so you will need 1, 2 or 3 steaks per serving according to the size of the fish.

PAN-FRIED SKATE WITH BALSAMIC VINEGAR

Serves 4

4 pieces of skate wing, each weighing about 200 g / 7 oz
125 ml / 4 fl oz / 1/2 cup balsamic vinegar
sea salt and freshly ground black pepper

3 tbsp vegetable oil
4 large handfuls of mixed salad leaves
3 tbsp Sherry Vinaigrette (see page 21)
fresh chervil leaves, to garnish

Arrange the pieces of skate in a shallow dish. Reserve 2 tbsp balsamic vinegar and pour the remainder over the fish. Cover the dish and refrigerate for 2–3 hours, turning the fish over from time to time.

Heat the oven to 200°C / 400°F / gas 6.

Remove the pieces of skate from the balsamic marinade and pat them dry with paper towels. Season them with a little salt and some pepper.

Heat a large frying pan over moderately high heat and add the oil. Pan-fry the skate for 2 minutes on each side. Transfer the fish to a shallow roasting pan, with the juices from the frying pan, and cover with buttered paper. Bake for about 8 minutes or until the fish is just cooked. Test with the point of a knife: the flesh in the centre should still be slightly translucent.

Meanwhile, wash and dry the salad leaves.

Remove the skate to warmed plates and sprinkle with the reserved balsamic vinegar. Toss the salad leaves with the vinaigrette, season with pepper and arrange on the plates. Give the fish a turn of the peppermill, garnish with chervil leaves and serve.

THAI CRAB CAKES

Serves 4

450 g / 1 lb white crab meat, preferably
   freshly cooked
1 stalk of lemon grass
100 g / 3¹/₂ oz spring onions [US scallions]
1-cm / ¹/₂-inch slice of fresh root ginger
3 small pickled gherkins or cornichons
5 tbsp Mayonnaise (see page 24)
90 g / 3 oz / 2 cups fine fresh white breadcrumbs
sea salt and freshly ground black pepper
1 egg
30 g / 1 oz / ¹/₃ cup flaked almonds
   [US sliced almonds]
3 tbsp groundnut oil [US peanut oil]
30 g / 1 oz / 2 tbsp unsalted butter
Thai Rice (see page 150), to serve
fresh coriander leaves [US cilantro], to garnish

For the sauce
1 small onion
¹/₂ garlic clove
4 fresh hot chilli peppers
1 stalk of lemon grass
1-cm / ¹/₂-inch slice of fresh root ginger
3 kaffir lime leaves
15 g / ¹/₂ oz / 1 tbsp unsalted butter
1 tbsp groundnut oil [US peanut oil]
100 ml / 3¹/₂ fl oz / 7 tbsp dry white wine
1 tsp tomato paste
400 ml / 14 fl oz / 1³/₄ cups double cream
   [US heavy whipping cream]
1 tbsp coconut cream
1 tbsp chopped fresh coriander [US cilantro]

Flake the crabmeat. Trim the lemon grass to remove all dry leaves, then chop finely. Trim and finely chop the spring onions. Peel the ginger and chop it finely. Finely chop the gherkins.

Combine all the prepared ingredients in a bowl and add the mayonnaise and 50 g / ³/₄ oz / 1 heaped cup of the breadcrumbs. Season. Mix well, divide into 8 portions and shape each into a 5.5-cm / 2¹/₄-inch diameter disc that is about 2.5 cm / 1 inch thick. Beat the egg in a shallow bowl. Dip the crab cakes in the egg, then coat with the remaining breadcrumbs. Refrigerate for 2 hours.

Meanwhile, make the sauce. Peel and finely chop the onion. Peel the garlic and chop to a paste (see page 13). Discard the core and seeds from the chillies and chop them finely. Trim and finely chop the lemon grass. Peel and finely chop the ginger. Chop the lime leaves.

Heat the butter and oil in a saucepan over low heat and add the onion, garlic, chillies, lemon grass, ginger and lime leaves. Cook until very soft, stirring occasionally. Stir in the wine and boil until reduced to a glaze. Add the tomato paste and cook for 1 minute longer, stirring. Stir in the cream and bring back to the boil. Boil for about 8 minutes or until reduced by one-quarter.

Purée the sauce in a blender, then press it through a fine sieve it into a clean pan. Stir in the coconut cream. Set aside.

Toast the almonds (see page 84).

Just before serving, heat a large frying pan over moderate heat and add the oil and butter. Fry the crab cakes for about 10 minutes or until they are golden brown on both sides. Drain on paper towels. Gently reheat the sauce, stir in the coriander and check the seasoning.

Spoon the hot Thai rice in the centre of each warmed plate and place the crab cakes on top. Pour the sauce around and sprinkle with toasted almonds and coriander leaves. Serve immediately.

TIPS

If you cannot get fresh lime leaves and lemon grass, you can use dried. Just soak in water overnight and drain well. An exotic addition to the crab cakes is 10 g / ¹/₃ oz of coriander roots, finely chopped.

You can substitute poached flaked white fish for the crabmeat.

The chilli-hot sauce also goes well with other fish dishes as well as with meat and poultry. If too hot for your taste, reduce the number of chillies used.

RIGHT
*Thai Crab Cakes
with Thai Rice*

GRILLED TUNA STEAK ON MIXED GREEN LEAVES WITH PINE NUTS

Serves 4

An ideal accompaniment for this dish is minted new potatoes (see recipe on page 142).

4 large handfuls of mixed green leaves such as rocket [US arugula], watercress and baby spinach, weighing about 120 g / 4 oz
2 ripe but firm plum tomatoes
30 g / 1 oz / ⅓ cup pine nuts
120 g / 4 oz streaky bacon [US Canadian bacon]

4 thick-cut tuna steaks, all skin and bones removed, each weighing about 140 g / 5 oz
sea salt and freshly ground black pepper
2 tbsp vegetable oil
juice of ½ lime
3½ tbsp Sherry Vinaigrette (see page 21)
4 tsp balsamic vinegar

Remove the stalks from the mixed green leaves. Wash and dry the leaves thoroughly. Peel the tomatoes and remove the seeds (see page 74). Cut the tomato flesh neatly into very small dice.

Heat the grill [US broiler].

Toast the pine nuts (see page 84).

Grill the bacon slices until crispy. Cut them across into fine strips and keep warm.

Season the tuna steaks with salt and pepper, then turn them in the oil to coat. Place them on the hot grill rack and grill for 4–6 minutes or until they just give and spring back when pressed with a finger in the middle. The steaks will be rare in the centre.

Meanwhile, toss the green leaves with the lime juice and vinaigrette. Divide the leaves among the plates.

Arrange the tuna steaks on the leaves. Sprinkle the strips of bacon, toasted pine nuts, and tomato dice on the leaves. Season to taste with salt and pepper, sprinkle over the balsamic vinegar, and serve.

TIPS

Be careful not to overcook the tuna or it will be dry. It must be cooked rare.

These tuna steaks are ideal for cooking on a charcoal grill, if the weather permits.

RIGHT
Grilled Tuna Steak on Mixed Green Leaves with Pine Nuts

GRILLED MACKEREL WITH GREEN PEAS AND BACON

Serves 4

The best time to make this dish is when green peas have just come into season. Use only small peas, and be sure they are well cooked.

1 small onion
30 g / 1 oz / 2 tbsp unsalted butter
300 g / 10 oz / 2 cups shelled fresh green peas
1 tsp sugar
400 ml / 14 fl oz / 1³/4 cups Chicken Essence (see page 14)
sea salt and freshly ground black pepper
100 g / 3¹/2 oz / 1 cup small button or baby onions [US pearl onions]

2 slices of streaky bacon [US Canadian bacon]
¹/2 head of round English lettuce [US butter-head lettuce]
15 g / ¹/2 oz / 1¹/2 tbsp flour
4 tbsp double cream [US heavy whipping cream]
fillets from 4 mackerel, each fish weighing about 350–450 g / ³/4 1 lb
2–3 tbsp groundnut oil [US peanut oil]
10 sprigs of fresh mint

Heat the grill [US broiler] and the grill pan with rack in place.

Peel and finely chop the small onion. Melt half the butter in a heavy-based saucepan over low heat and cook the chopped onion until soft and translucent, stirring often. Add the peas and sugar and cook gently for 1 minute longer.

Add the chicken essence and season with salt and pepper. Bring to the boil, then reduce the heat, cover and simmer gently for 10 minutes or until the peas are tender.

Meanwhile, peel the onions and cook in boiling salted water until tender; drain. Grill the bacon until crisp and browned; cut it across into fine strips. Wash the lettuce and dry well, then cut into fine strips. With a fork, mash the remaining butter with the flour until well blended.

Add the butter and flour mixture to the peas and cook, stirring, until the liquid has thickened. Stir in the button onions, bacon and cream. Keep warm.

Season the fish fillets and turn them in the oil to coat both sides. Arrange on the hot grill rack and grill for about 3 minutes or until just cooked, turning once. Test with the point of a knife: the flesh in the centre should still be slightly translucent.

While the fish is cooking, pull the mint leaves from the stalks and wash and dry them. Chop the leaves.

Stir the lettuce and mint into the peas, taste and adjust the seasoning. Serve the fish and peas on warmed plates. Give the fish a turn of the peppermill and serve immediately.

TIPS

If fresh green peas are not in season, you can use frozen peas. Cook them for 4–5 minutes, from frozen.

The pea and bacon mixture, without the cream, can be served as a vegetable with many other main dishes.

SEA BREAM ON
AN AUBERGINE PURÉE

Serves 4

Fresh rosemary adds a beautiful perfume here.

fillets from 4 scaled sea bream [US porgy], each fish weighing 350–450 g / 3/4 1 lb
sea salt and freshly ground black pepper
2 tbsp groundnut oil [US peanut oil]
200 ml / 7 fl oz / 7/8 cup Sun-Dried Tomato Sauce (see page 17)
30 g / 1 oz / 2 tbsp unsalted butter
4 large sprigs of fresh rosemary

For the aubergine purée
2 aubergines [US eggplants], weighing about 500 g / 1 lb 2 oz
2 garlic cloves
5 tbsp groundnut oil [US peanut oil]
1/2 tsp ground cumin
2 tbsp crème fraîche or double cream [US heavy whipping cream]

First make the aubergine purée. Peel the aubergines and cut the flesh into cubes. Peel the garlic and chop to a paste (see page 13).

Heat the oil in a heavy-based saucepan over low heat and cook the garlic for 30 seconds, stirring. Add the aubergines and cumin and season with salt and pepper. Cover and cook gently for about 15 minutes, stirring from time to time, until very soft and mushy.

Drain the aubergine cubes in a colander and allow to cool slightly, then purée in a blender or food processor. Transfer to a saucepan and set aside.

Heat the grill [US broiler] and the grill pan with rack in place.

Season the sea bream fillets and turn them in the oil to coat all sides. Arrange the fillets on the hot grill rack, skin side down, and grill for about 2 minutes. Turn and cook for a further 1 minute. Test with the point of a knife: the flesh in the centre should still be slightly translucent.

Meanwhile, reheat the aubergine purée and stir in the cream. Taste and adjust the seasoning.

Divide the aubergine purée among warmed plates and place the fish fillets on top. Spoon the sun-dried tomato sauce around. Keep hot.

Melt the butter in a small pan and add the rosemary sprigs. Cook, swirling the butter around in the pan, until it is lightly browned. Put a rosemary sprig on top of each serving and spoon over the browned butter. Give the fish a turn of the peppermill and serve immediately.

SCALLOPS IN BACON WITH SAGE

Serves 4

This is one of my favourite dishes. The thinly sliced smoked bacon and the fresh sage contrast beautifully with the sweet flavour of scallops.

12 or 16 large scallops [US sea scallops]
without the roe (coral), weighing about
700 g / 1¹/₂ lb
sea salt and freshly ground black pepper
12 or 16 very thin slices of smoked streaky
bacon [US Canadian bacon]

12 or 16 fresh sage leaves
15 g / ¹/₂ oz / 1 tbsp unsalted butter
3 tbsp groundnut oil [US peanut oil]
Potato Ratatouille (see page 140), to serve
200 ml / 7 fl oz / ⁷/₈ cup Sun-Dried Tomato
Sauce (see page 17)

Trim the hard, greyish-white gristly bit from each scallop, leaving just the tender white nut of meat. Put the scallops in a bowl of iced water and leave for 10 minutes to firm up.

Drain the scallops and dry with paper towels. Season with salt and pepper. Trim rind from the bacon. Put a sage leaf on each scallop, then wrap in a slice of bacon and secure with a wooden cocktail stick.

Heat a frying pan over moderate heat and add half the butter and the oil. Fry the bacon-wrapped scallops for about 4 minutes or until the bacon is crisp and golden brown on all sides. Add the remaining butter to the pan when you turn the scallops over. Drain on paper towels and remove the cocktail sticks.

Spoon the potato ratatouille in the centre of warmed plates and place the bacon-wrapped scallops on top. Give the fish a turn of the peppermill. Pour the sun-dried tomato sauce around and serve.

TIP

If you cannot get thin slices of bacon, flatten the slices between sheets of cling film [US plastic wrap] until they are paper thin.

RIGHT
Scallops in Bacon
with Sage

HERRING FILLETS IN A MUSTARD CRUST WITH ONION RINGS

Serves 4

An excellent accompaniment for this savoury dish is new potatoes cooked in their skins, dressed with butter and fresh mint (see recipe on page 142).

2 tbsp whole-grain mustard
60 g / 2 oz / 1¹/₃ cups fresh white breadcrumbs
2 tbsp chopped fresh parsley
2 tbsp olive oil
sea salt and freshly ground black pepper
fillets from 4 plump herrings

For the bean and tomato salad
225 g / 8 oz French beans [US fine green beans]
2 shallots

1 small garlic clove
3–4 tbsp Sherry Vinaigrette (see page 21)
4 ripe but firm plum tomatoes

For the onion rings
vegetable oil for deep-frying
2 onions
a little milk
flour for coating

First make the bean and tomato salad. Trim the ends from the beans, then cook them in boiling salted water for 3–4 minutes or until they are just tender but still firm. Drain and refresh in iced water, then drain again well. Dry the beans on paper towels and cut them across in half.

Peel and finely chop the shallots. Peel the garlic and chop to a paste (see page 13). Combine the beans, shallots and garlic in a bowl and add the vinaigrette. Toss to dress the vegetables.

Peel the tomatoes (see page 74). Cut the flesh into neat wedges and add to the bowl. Season with salt and pepper. Toss gently to mix. Set aside.

Heat the grill [US broiler] and the grill pan with rack in place. Heat a pan of oil for deep-frying to 180°C / 350°F.

Mix together the mustard, breadcrumbs, parsley and enough olive oil to bind. Season with salt and pepper. For the onion rings, peel the onions and cut them into 5-mm / ¼-inch slices. Separate the slices into rings and select the large ones for deep frying.

Season the herring fillets with salt and pepper, then turn them in olive oil to coat all over. Arrange the fillets on the hot grill rack, skin side down, and grill for 2 minutes.

Turn the fillets over and spread the mustard mixture evenly over the skin. Return to the heat and grill for about 3 minutes longer or until the mustard crust is golden brown and the fish is cooked. Test with the point of a knife: the flesh in the centre should still be slightly translucent.

While the fish is grilling, prepare the onion rings: dip them in milk and then into seasoned flour, shaking off the excess. Fry in the hot oil for about 2 minutes, turning once, or until golden brown all over. Drain on paper towels.

Transfer the herring fillets to warmed plates and give them a turn of the peppermill. Garnish with the onion rings. Serve the bean and tomato salad on the side.

SWEET PEPPERS FILLED WITH SALT COD AND BASIL

Serves 4

A dish from the sunny coasts of Spain and Portugal, this has a unique strong and earthy flavour. It leaves a lingering, satisfying taste.

300 g / 10 oz salt cod fillet
milk and water for soaking cod
8 small, squat sweet peppers, preferably 4 red and 4 yellow
50 g / 1 3/4 oz / 1 cup fresh basil leaves
2 garlic cloves
4 tbsp extra virgin olive oil
500 ml / 16 fl oz / 2 cups milk
100 ml / 3 1/2 fl oz / 7 tbsp double cream [US heavy whipping cream]

freshly ground black pepper
300 g / 10 oz potatoes
60 g / 2 oz / 1/3 cup black olives
150 ml / 1/4 pint / 2/3 cup Sherry Vinaigrette (see page 21)
4 tbsp chopped mixed fresh herbs such as chives, parsley, basil and dill

Put the salt cod in a bowl, cover with half milk and half water, and soak for 24 hours, changing the milk and water three times. Drain. Remove and discard the skin and bones.

Heat the oven to 220°C / 425°F / gas 7. Line the bottom of a roasting pan with foil and heat in the oven.

Cut the tops off the peppers; reserve the tops. Remove the seeds and white ribs. If necessary, cut a thin slice from the base of each pepper so it will stand upright. Be careful not to cut a hole in the pepper base.

Chop the basil leaves and peeled garlic and put into the peppers. Brush the outsides and tops of the peppers with a little olive oil, then arrange in the hot roasting pan. Cover with a lid or foil and bake for 20 minutes.

Scrape the garlic and basil out of the peppers into a saucepan. Leave the peppers, covered, to cool.

Add the salt cod to the saucepan together with the measured quantity of milk, half the cream, and 1 tbsp olive oil. Season with

pepper. Simmer for about 40 minutes or until the cod is very soft.

Peel the potatoes and cut into cubes. Cook in boiling water, without salt, until tender, then drain.

When the peppers and the lids are cool enough to handle, peel them.

Drain the liquid from the salt cod and put the cod mixture in a food processor with the potatoes. Process for just a few seconds. With the motor running, slowly add the remaining cream and olive oil through the feed tube.

Turn the oven down to 200°C / 400°F / gas 6. Fill the peppers with the salt cod mixture and replace the tops. Set them in a roasting pan in which they will just fit. Cover and heat in the oven for 20 minutes.

Remove the stones [US pits] from the olives and slice them.

Gently heat the vinaigrette until lukewarm, stirring constantly. Add the herbs and black olives.

Put 2 peppers on each warmed plate. Pour vinaigrette around peppers and serve.

OVER PAGE
Sweet Peppers Filled with Salt Cod and Basil

POACHED FILLETS OF COD ON OLIVE OIL AND HERB POTATOES

Serves 4

500 ml / 16 fl oz / 2 cups milk
1 small onion
1/2 bay leaf
1 whole clove
sea salt and freshly ground black pepper

2 eggs
4 pieces of skinned cod fillet, each weighing
    150–175 g / 5–6 oz
4 tbsp chopped fresh chives
Olive Oil Potatoes (see page 141)

Combine the milk and 250 ml / 8 fl oz / 1 cup of water in a wide pan. Peel the onion. Secure the bay leaf to the onion with the clove and add to the pan. Season. Heat to simmering point, then remove and set aside.

Put the eggs in a pan of boiling water, bring back to the boil and cook for 6 minutes. Drain the eggs and run cold water over them to cool the shells quickly. Peel the eggs and keep them warm.

Bring the milk mixture back to simmering point, then turn the heat down so the liquid is barely moving. Add the cod fillets and poach for about 4 minutes or until just cooked. Test with the point of a knife: the flesh in the centre should still be slightly translucent. Lift the fillets out of the liquid and drain them on paper towels.

Stir half the chives into the potatoes. Spoon on to warmed plates and top with the fish. Give the fish a turn of the peppermill. Roughly chop the eggs and mix with the remaining chives. Place on top of the fish and serve immediately.

TIPS

For all fish dishes, I recommend that you season with freshly ground sea salt.

Should you like a little sauce with this, chicken concentrate (see recipe on page 16) would go nicely.

DEEP FRIED HALIBUT ON WARM POTATO SALAD

Serves 4

1 small head of curly endive
1 small head of radicchio
vegetable oil for deep frying
4 pieces of skinned halibut fillet,
    each weighing about 150 g / 5 oz
sea salt and freshly ground black pepper

flour for coating
300 ml / 1/2 pint / 1 1/4 cups White Batter
    (see page 18)
Warm Potato Salad (see page 141), to serve
4 tbsp Sherry Vinaigrette (see page 21)

Separate the curly endive and radicchio leaves. Wash and dry them well.

Heat oil for deep frying to 180°C / 350°F. Dry the halibut fillets with paper towels. Season. Coat lightly on both sides with flour, shaking off excess. Dip the fillets into the batter, then lower them into the hot oil. Fry for about 5 minutes or until golden brown on both sides. Drain on paper towels.

Spoon the potato salad on to warmed plates and place the fish on top. Give the fish a turn of the peppermill. Quickly toss the endive and radicchio leaves in the vinaigrette, arrange around the potato salad, and serve.

TIPS

Make the potato salad before frying the fish. It can be kept warm for at least 20 minutes.

The fish is cooked when it 'swims' in the oil, and should be served immediately.

GRILLED BREAST OF CHICKEN IN MUSTARD AND CORIANDER SAUCE

Serves 4

This light and very pleasant dish is best made in late spring and early summer when leeks are young and juicy.

TIP

If you like, you can remove the bones from the chicken breasts before spreading them with mustard.

4 chicken breasts with wings attached [US chicken breast halves], each weighing about 250 g / 9 oz
salt and freshly ground black pepper
4 tbsp groundnut oil [US peanut oil]
400 g / 14 oz leeks, white and pale green parts only

45 g / 1 1/2 oz / 3 tbsp unsalted butter
about 3 tbsp coarse-grain mustard
1 onion
200 ml / 7 fl oz / 7/8 cup Chicken Concentrate (see page 16)
4 tbsp double cream [US heavy whipping cream]
8 sprigs of fresh coriander [US cilantro]

Heat the grill [US broiler] and the grill pan with rack in place.

Season the chicken breasts with salt and pepper, then turn them in 2 tbsp of oil to coat all over. Set them skin side up on the hot rack in the grill pan and grill under moderate heat (or about 7.5 cm / 3 inches from the heat) for 15–20 minutes or until golden brown and cooked through. Turn the breasts over halfway through the cooking.

Meanwhile, trim the leeks, cut them lengthwise in half and wash well. Cut across into 5-mm / 1/4-inch slices. Heat 15 g / 1/2 oz / 1 tbsp of the butter and 1 tbsp oil in a heavy-based saucepan over low heat. Add the leeks and season with salt and pepper. Cover and cook for about 5 minutes or until the leeks are tender, stirring occasionally.

About 5 minutes before the chicken breasts have finished cooking, turn them skin side up again and brush with a little of the mustard. Increase the heat to high (or move them closer to the heat) to glaze the surface.

Peel and finely chop the onion. Heat the remaining butter and oil in another saucepan over low heat and cook the onion until soft and translucent, stirring often. Add the chicken concentrate and cream and bring to the boil. Boil for 2–3 minutes or until slightly reduced and thickened.

Strain the sauce through a fine sieve. Chop the coriander leaves and stir into the sauce with the remaining mustard. Taste and adjust the seasoning and keep warm.

Spoon the leeks into the centre of warmed plates and place a chicken breast on top. Spoon the sauce around the chicken and serve immediately.

STUFFED CHICKEN WITH ROASTED VEGETABLES

Serves 4

This is a simple dish, yet very tasty. You never get tired of eating it. Choose 3 or 4 vegetables to roast with the chicken. My suggestions would be parsnips, red sweet peppers, courgettes [US zucchini] and celeriac [US root celery]. Be sure to put garlic in the roasting pan, for flavour and aroma.

1 large onion
2 garlic cloves
15 g / 1/2 oz / 1 tbsp unsalted butter
100 ml / 3 1/2 fl oz / 7 tbsp groundnut oil
   [US peanut oil]
45 g / 1 1/2 oz / 1/4 cup black olives
150 g / 5 oz / 3 cups fine fresh white
   breadcrumbs
grated zest of 1 unwaxed orange
grated zest of 1 unwaxed lemon

3 tbsp chopped fresh coriander [US cilantro]
salt and freshly ground black pepper
1 egg
2 chickens, each weighing about 1.2 kg / 2 1/2 lb
Roasted Vegetables with Rosemary
   (see page 143)
100 ml / 3 1/2 fl oz / 7 tbsp dry white wine
300 ml / 1/2 pint / 1 1/4 cups Chicken
   Concentrate (see page 16)
fresh herbs, to garnish

Peel and finely chop the onion. Peel the garlic and chop to a paste (see page 13). Heat the butter and 2 tbsp of the oil in a small frying pan over low heat and cook the onion until soft, stirring often. Add the garlic and cook for 1 minute longer. Remove from the heat and allow to cool.

Remove the stones [US pits] from the olives, roughly chop them and put in a bowl. Add the breadcrumbs, onion and garlic mixture, orange and lemon zests, and fresh coriander. Season. Beat the egg and add to the bowl. Mix all the ingredients.

Heat the oven to 200°C / 400°F / gas 6.

Season the chickens, inside and out. Divide the olive stuffing between them and pack it into the body cavity. Secure the cavity opening with a skewer and tie the ends of the legs together with string.

Heat a large roasting pan on top of the stove and add the remaining oil. Turn the chickens in the hot oil to coat, then turn the birds on their sides. Transfer to the oven and roast for 30 minutes, turning the birds on to their other sides halfway through the cooking. Turn the birds on to their backs and roast for a further 30 minutes, basting frequently with the hot oil.

Add the vegetables to the roasting pan according to their roasting times.

Remove the chickens and vegetables from the roasting pan and keep warm. Pour the fat from the pan. Add the wine and set the pan over high heat on top of the stove. Bring to the boil, stirring well to scrape the browned bits from the pan base. Boil until reduced by half.

Add the chicken concentrate and simmer for 2 minutes. Adjust the seasoning, then strain the gravy through a fine sieve.

Cut the chickens into neat pieces and serve with the olive stuffing, roasted vegetables and gravy. You could also serve bread sauce (see page 116 for recipe).

RIGHT
Stuffed Chicken with Roasted Vegetables

THE SAVOY'S CHICKEN PIE

Serves 4

This simple yet delicious dish brings out the deep, rich flavour of chicken. It is ideal for entertaining because there is very little to do at the end.

2 chickens, each weighing about 1 kg / 2¼ lb
2 onions
200 g / 7 oz button mushrooms
45 g / 1½ oz / 3 tbsp unsalted butter
salt and freshly ground black pepper
500 ml / 16 fl oz / 2 cups Chicken Essence
    (see page 14)

1 tbsp chopped mixed fresh tarragon and parsley
4 slices of back bacon [US Canadian bacon]
2 hard-boiled eggs
400 g / 14 oz Puff Pastry (see page 27)
1 egg yolk

TIP
Olive oil potatoes (see recipe on page 141) would go very well with the pie.

Cut the legs off the chickens and shape them into neat 'butterflies' (see box). Remove the wingtips and wishbone and take the breasts off the chickens.

Peel and finely chop the onions. Trim and quarter the mushrooms. Melt the butter in a saucepan over low heat and cook the onions until soft and translucent, stirring often. Add the mushrooms and season. Cook for 1 minute longer, stirring.

Season the chicken legs and add them to the pan. Pour in the chicken essence. Bring to the boil, then reduce the heat and simmer for about 20 minutes.

Add the chicken breasts and continue simmering for 10 minutes.

Remove the chicken from the pan and set aside to cool. Increase the heat and boil the cooking liquid for about 10 minutes or until it has reduced by about one-third. Remove from the heat and season. Allow to cool, then stir in the herbs.

Remove any rind from the bacon, then wrap the chicken breasts in the bacon slices. Shell the hard-boiled eggs and cut them in half. Arrange the chicken breasts and legs and egg halves in a deep 1.8-litre / 3-pint / 2-quart pie dish or baking dish.

Taste the cooking liquid for seasoning, then pour it into the dish.

Roll out the puff pastry dough to an oval or round (according to the shape of the pie dish) that is 8.5 cm / 3½ inches larger than the top of the dish. Lay the dough over the pie dish, leaving the dough to hang evenly over the edges. Lightly beat the egg yolk with 1 tsp water and brush this egg wash over the pastry dough. Allow it to dry, then brush the dough with egg wash again. Leave to rest in a cool place for 15 minutes.

Heat the oven to 190°C / 375°F /gas 5.

Bake the pie for 40 minutes or until the pastry is risen and golden brown.

If you like, use a sharp knife to trim off the excess pastry before serving.

Illustrated on page 15

TO SHAPE A CHICKEN LEG 'BUTTERFLY'
If there is a knuckle bone, twist it off. Cut through the skin around the leg bone about 4 cm / 1½ inches from the end of the drumstick, then remove the skin to expose the bone at the end of the drumstick. Make a lengthwise cut in the thigh, to the bone, and cut around the ball and socket joint between the thigh and drumstick. Neatly cut out the thigh bone and the joint (keep these for making chicken concentrate, page 16). Make an incision in the far end of the thigh meat and push the exposed end of the drumstick bone through it.

CHILLED SUMMER CHICKEN WITH BLACK OLIVES AND SULTANAS

Serves 4

2 chickens, each weighing about 900 g / 2 lb
120 g / 4 oz button onions [US pearl onions]
60 g / 2 oz small button mushrooms
4 young carrots
2 young leeks, white and pale green parts only
1/2 celery stalk
10 sprigs of fresh tarragon
3 tbsp olive oil

salt and freshly ground black pepper
300 ml / 1/2 pint / 1 1/4 cups dry white wine
250 ml / 8 fl oz / 1 cup white wine vinegar
900 ml / 1 1/2 pints / 3 3/4 cups Chicken
  Essence (see page 14)
20 black olives, weighing about 75 g / 2 1/2 oz
60 g / 2 oz / 1/3 cup sultanas [US golden
  raisins]

Cut the chickens into pieces (see box), or have your butcher do this for you. Remove all the skin from the chicken pieces.

Peel the onions. Trim off the mushroom stalks. If any mushrooms are larger than the others, cut them in half. Peel and slice the carrots. Trim the leeks, cut in half and wash well, then cut across into 5-mm / 1/4-inch slices. Peel the celery and cut across into thin slices. Pull the tarragon leaves from the stalks; set both leaves and stalks aside.

Heat a heavy-based pan over moderate heat and add the oil. Season the chicken pieces and fry until lightly coloured all over. Do this in batches if necessary. Add the onions, mushrooms, carrots, leeks and celery and fry for 1 minute longer, stirring well.

Add the wine, vinegar and enough chicken essence to cover the chicken pieces. Add the tarragon stalks. Bring to the boil, then simmer very gently for about 20 minutes. As the vegetables are cooked (just tender but still firm), remove them with a slotted spoon and set aside.

When the chicken has finished cooking, lift out the pieces and put them in a serving dish with the vegetables. Boil the cooking liquid until reduced by one-quarter, then strain it. Chop the tarragon leaves and stir into the liquid. Season with salt and pepper. Pour the liquid over the chicken and vegetables (there should be enough liquid to cover the chicken completely). Stir in the olives and sultanas and leave to cool, then taste and adjust the seasoning.

Cover the dish and refrigerate overnight. The cooking liquid will set into a light jelly.

Serve this summer dish with minted new potatoes (see recipe on page 142) and a green salad.

TO CUT A CHICKEN INTO PIECES

Use a sharp chef's knife. Cut off the legs by severing the joint between the thigh and body carcass. Sever the joint between the thigh and drumstick. If necessary, twist off the gristly end, or knuckle bone, from each drumstick. Sever the second wing joint to separate the wingtip and first wing section from the second wing section (which is still attached to the carcass). Separate the whole breast from the back by cutting through the flap of skin, just below the rib cage on either side, and then through the joints, pulling the breast and back apart with your hands as you cut. Cut through the cartilage on the underside of the breast-bone, then place the breast skin side up and press down hard to break the bone. Cut the breast in half. Trim all the pieces. You will now have 2 drumsticks, 2 thighs, and 2 breast portions with single wing sections attached. Reserve the back and wing tip sections for making chicken concentrate (see recipe on page 16).

POACHED CHICKEN IN A TARRAGON CREAM SAUCE

Serves 4

2 chickens, each weighing about 900 g / 2 lb
8 sprigs of fresh tarragon
2.5 litres / 4 pints / 2¹/₂ quarts Chicken Essence (see page 14)
salt and freshly ground black pepper
450 g / 1 lb mixed vegetables such as celery or

celeriac [US celery root], carrots, green beans, small leeks, turnips
45 g / 1¹/₂ oz / 3 tbsp unsalted butter
4 tsp flour
150 ml / ¹/₄ pint / ²/₃ cup crème fraîche or double cream [US heavy whipping cream]

Remove the wishbone from each chicken, then truss the birds. Put them in a large pot. Pull the leaves from the tarragon stalks; set the leaves aside. Add the stalks to the chicken. Pour in enough chicken essence to cover the chickens and season with salt and pepper. Bring to the boil, skimming well. Simmer for about 25 minutes or until the chickens are cooked. Test by inserting a skewer into the thigh meat: the juice that runs out should be clear.

Prepare the vegetables. Trim celery. Peel celeriac, carrots and turnips. Cut these vegetables into 5-mm / ¹/₄-inch sticks that are 4 cm / 1¹/₂ inches long. Trim leeks and wash well. Cut across into 5-cm / 2-inch pieces. Trim green beans and cut in half.

When the chickens are cooked, lift them out of the liquid and set aside to cool slightly. Strain the essence into a clean saucepan and bring back to the boil. Cook the prepared vegetables in the essence until they are just tender but still firm, then remove from essence and set aside. Keep the essence hot.

Cut the legs from the chickens. Make a lengthwise cut in the underside of each thigh, to the bone, then cut through the joint between the thigh and drumstick to

sever it. Remove and discard the thigh bone. Cut the breasts off the chickens, cutting close to the rib cage to remove neat boneless pieces. When you reach the joint between the wing and carcass, sever it to keep the wing attached to the breast. Set the chicken pieces in a dish, spoon over a little essence and keep warm.

Melt half of the butter in a heavy-based saucepan over low heat. Add the flour and cook for 2 minutes, stirring constantly. Remove from the heat and allow to cool a little, then gradually stir in 350 ml / 12 fl oz / 1¹/₂ cups of the hot chicken essence. Return to the heat and bring to the boil, whisking constantly. When the sauce has thickened slightly, whisk in the cream. Simmer for about 10 minutes, whisking often.

Chop the tarragon leaves. Melt the remaining butter in another pan and toss the vegetables to reheat them. Season with salt and pepper.

Strain the sauce through a fine sieve and stir in the chopped tarragon. Taste and adjust the seasoning.

Place the pieces of chicken on warmed plates and spoon the sauce over them. Arrange the vegetables and mushrooms over and around the chicken and serve.

TIPS

If you like, add 100 g / 3¹/₂ oz fresh wild or small button mushrooms. Trim the stalks. Melt a little butter in a small pan and cook the mushrooms until they are tender and the liquid they exude has evaporated, stirring occasionally. Arrange on the chicken with the vegetables.

The tarragon must be very fresh because it is the dominating flavour in this tasty dish, and it must be chopped at the last minute so it does not dry up and lose its pungency.

Be sure to keep all the bones for making chicken concentrate (see recipe on page 16).

TURKEY MEDALLIONS WRAPPED IN PARMA HAM ON BEANS

Serves 4

8 slices of turkey breast, each weighing about
   75 g / 2¹/2 oz
salt and freshly ground black pepper
16 fresh sage leaves
8 slices of Parma ham
90 g / 3 oz each French beans [US thin green
   beans] and podded fresh young broad beans
   [US fava beans]

45 g / 1¹/2 oz / 3 tbsp unsalted butter
2 tbsp groundnut oil [US peanut oil]
100 ml / 3¹/2 fl oz / 7 tbsp dry white wine
200 ml / 7 fl oz / ⁷/8 cup Chicken Concentrate
   (see page 16)
White Bean Stew (see page 149), made
   without the tomato paste

Place the slices of turkey between sheets of cling film [US plastic wrap] and pound them gently until they are about 5-mm / ¹/4-inch thick. Do not make holes in the turkey. Trim the edges to neaten them, if necessary.

Season these turkey medallions with pepper and a little salt. Put 2 sage leaves on top of each medallion and cover with a slice of Parma ham, folding under the edges if necessary so the ham is the same size as the turkey. Secure the sage and ham to the turkey with wooden cocktail sticks.

Trim the green beans and cut them across in half. Blanch the green beans and broad beans in boiling salted water for 2 minutes, then drain. Refresh in iced water and drain again well. Set aside.

Heat two-thirds of the butter and all the oil in a large frying pan over moderately high heat and fry the medallions for 1 minute on each side or until golden brown and cooked through. Remove from the pan and keep hot.

Pour off all the fat from the pan. Add the wine and bring to the boil. Boil until reduced by half. Stir in the chicken concentrate and bring back to the boil. Simmer until slightly thickened. Taste and adjust the seasoning.

Heat the remaining butter in a small pan and toss the green and broad beans until heated through. Stir into the white bean stew. Spoon on to the centre of the warmed plates.

Remove the cocktail sticks from the medallions and arrange them on the beans. Pour the sauce around and serve immediately.

SLOW-ROASTED ORIENTAL DUCK

Serves 4

Although it may seem an unusual combination, the duck is superb served on top of spoonfuls of lentil ragoût.

2 ducks, each weighing about 1.5 kg / 3¹/₂ lb
2 garlic cloves
1 tbsp finely chopped fresh root ginger
3¹/₂ tbsp soy sauce
100 ml / 3¹/₂ fl oz / 7 tbsp honey
vegetable oil for deep frying

2 handfuls of rocket leaves [US arugula]

For serving
Lentil Ragoût (see page 51)
Vegetable Spring Rolls (see page 147)

Bring a large pot of salted water to the boil. One at a time, immerse the ducks in the boiling water and blanch for 15 minutes. Drain, pat dry with paper towels and set aside to cool.

Heat the oven to 100°C / 210°F / gas very low.

Using a fork or skewer, pierce the skin of the ducks all over the breast and legs (don't prick through the flesh). Place the ducks on a rack in a roasting pan.

Peel the garlic and chop to a paste (see page 13). Mix the garlic with the ginger, soy sauce and honey in a bowl. Brush the ducks all over with this mixture, then roast for 3 hours. Brush the ducks every 15 minutes with the ginger mixture.

At the end of 3 hours, remove the ducks from the oven and turn the temperature up to its highest setting. Return the ducks to the oven and roast for 5–10 minutes to crisp the skin.

Heat a pan of oil for deep frying to 200°C / 400°F.

Cut the legs and boneless breasts off the ducks. Arrange them on warmed plates with the lentil ragoût and spring rolls. Keep hot.

Quickly deep fry the rocket leaves for 30 seconds or until they are crisp and bright green. Drain on paper towels and sprinkle over the duck. Serve immediately.

PHEASANT ON COUSCOUS

Serves 4

2 pheasants, with their breasts dressed with thin slices of bacon
salt and freshly ground black pepper
20 g / 2/3 oz / 4 tsp unsalted butter
3 tbsp groundnut oil [US peanut oil]
1 small onion

1 garlic clove
4 tbsp dry white wine
300 ml / 1/2 pint / 1 1/4 cups Chicken Concentrate (see page 16)
Sophie's Couscous (see page 151), made with the livers from the pheasants if available

Heat the oven to 200°C / 400°F / gas 6.

Remove the wishbone from each pheasant. Season the birds with salt and pepper. Heat a heavy-based roasting pan on top of the stove. Add the butter and oil and then the pheasants to the pan and turn the birds to coat with the fat. Turn the birds on to one side. Transfer the pan to the oven and roast for 20 minutes, turning the birds on to their other sides halfway through. Turn the birds breast up and remove the bacon; put the bacon in the roasting pan around the pheasants. Continue roasting the birds for 10–15 minutes, basting frequently with the fat and juices in the pan. Remove the bacon as soon as it is crisp.

Meanwhile, peel and finely chop the onion. Peel the garlic and chop to a paste (see page 13).

Remove the pheasants and crisp bacon to a carving board and set aside in a warm place to rest for about 10 minutes.

Pour the fat from the roasting pan. Add the onion and set the pan over low heat on top of the stove. Cook until soft and translucent, stirring often. Add the garlic and cook for 1 minute longer. Stir in the white wine and bring to the boil. Boil until reduced by two-thirds.

Meanwhile, cut the legs from the pheasants and separate the thighs and drumsticks. Make a lengthwise cut in the underside of each thigh, to the bone, then cut around the thigh bone and discard it. Cut the breasts off the pheasants, cutting close to the rib cage to remove neat boneless pieces. When you reach the joint between the wing and carcass, sever it to keep the wing attached to the breast. Set the breasts and thighs aside with the bacon, covered with buttered paper, in a warm place (the turned-off oven if available). Chop the pheasant carcasses and the drumsticks.

Stir the chicken concentrate into the wine reduction and bring to the boil. Add the chopped carcasses and drumsticks and simmer for about 7 minutes. Strain through a fine sieve or strainer lined with muslin [US cheesecloth], pressing down on the bones and vegetables to extract the maximum liquid and flavour. Taste and adjust the seasoning.

Spoon the couscous on to the warmed plates. Slice each pheasant breast into 3, at an angle, and arrange on the plates with the thighs and crisp bacon. Pour the sauce around and serve immediately.

PIGEON ON A PURÉE OF BRUSSELS SPROUTS

Serves 4

4 pigeons [US squab], with their breasts
    dressed with thin slices of bacon
salt and freshly ground black pepper
3 tbsp vegetable oil
1 small onion
1 carrot
1 celery stalk
1 small leek, white and pale green parts only
4 tbsp dry white wine
1/2 tsp black peppercorns

1/2 bay leaf
1 sprig of fresh thyme
200 ml / 7 fl oz / 7/8 cup Chicken Concentrate
    (see page 16)
watercress sprigs, to garnish

For serving
Purée of Brussels Sprouts (see page 149)
Bread Sauce (see box)

Heat the oven to 220°C / 425°F / gas 7.

Season the pigeons with salt and pepper. Heat a roasting pan on top of the stove. Add the pigeons and oil to the pan and turn the birds to coat with oil. Turn the birds on to one side. Transfer the pan to the oven and roast for 8 minutes, turning the birds on to their other sides after 4 minutes. Turn the birds breast up and remove the bacon; put the bacon in the roasting pan around the pigeons. Continue roasting the birds for 4 minutes, basting frequently with the oil and juices in the pan. Remove the pigeons and crisp bacon to a carving board and set aside in a warm place to rest for 5 minutes.

Cut the breasts and legs neatly from the pigeons and set them aside with the bacon, covered with buttered paper, in a warm place. Chop the pigeon carcasses and put them back in the roasting pan. Roast for a further 10 minutes or until the bones are lightly coloured.

Meanwhile, peel the onion and carrot. Trim the celery. Trim the leek, cut it in half lengthwise and wash thoroughly. Chop all the vegetables.

Add the vegetables to the roasting pan and stir well. Roast for a further 5 minutes.

Set the pan over high heat on top of the stove. Stir in the wine and bring to the boil. Lightly crush the peppercorns with the base of a small heavy pan and add to the roasting pan with the herbs. Boil, stirring well, until the liquid has reduced by half.

Add the chicken concentrate and simmer for about 10 minutes, stirring frequently. Strain the sauce through a fine sieve into a saucepan, pressing on the vegetables and seasonings to extract the maximum flavour and liquid. Skim off excess fat and impurities. Taste and adjust the seasoning and keep hot.

Place 2 spoonfuls of Brussels sprouts purée in a round in the middle of each warmed plate and arrange the pieces of pigeon on top. Set the crisp bacon on the breasts. Pour the sauce around and garnish with watercress. Serve immediately, with bread sauce.

TIPS

You can prepare partridge or pheasant in the same way.

Ask your butcher to remove the wishbone from the pigeons as this makes it easier to take off the breasts after roasting.

As soon as the oven is turned off, after roasting the bones and vegetables, put the pigeon pieces and bacon back in the oven to keep them warm.

RIGHT
Partridge on a Purée of Brussels Sprouts

BREAD SAUCE

With a whole clove, secure a bay leaf to 1/2 peeled onion. Combine the onion and 450 ml / 3/4 pint / nearly 2 cups milk in a saucepan and slowly bring to the boil. Remove and discard the onion, then stir 100 g / 3 1/2 oz / 2 1/4 cups fresh white breadcrumbs into the hot milk. Season with salt and pepper. Stir in 30 g / 1 oz / 2 tbsp unsalted butter until melted, then serve.

ANTON EDELMANN CREATIVE CUISINE

RABBIT WITH SPINACH AND APRICOTS

Serves 4

75 g / 2¹/2 oz / nearly ¹/2 cup dried apricots
2 onions
2 garlic cloves
450 g / 1 lb fresh spinach
4 rabbit leg portions, each weighing about
   170 g / 6 oz
80 g / 2³/4 oz / 5¹/2 tbsp unsalted butter
4 tbsp groundnut oil [US peanut oil]
salt and freshly ground black pepper
6 sprigs of fresh tarragon

1 tsp black peppercorns
100 ml / 3¹/2 fl oz / 7 tbsp dry white wine
200 ml / 7 fl oz / ⁷/8 cup Chicken Concentrate
   (see page 16)
100 ml / 3¹/2 fl oz / 7 tbsp double cream
   [US heavy whipping cream]
4 tbsp freshly grated horseradish or 8 tbsp
   creamed horseradish
freshly grated nutmeg
Sauté Potatoes (see page 140), to serve

Put the apricots in a bowl, cover with cold water and set aside to soak for 30 minutes.

Peel and finely chop the onions. Peel the garlic and chop to a paste (see page 13). Pull the stalks off the spinach. Blanch the leaves in boiling water for 30 seconds, drain and refresh in iced water. Drain again and squeeze all excess water. Chop one-third of the spinach; leave the remainder as whole leaves.

Part bone each rabbit leg (see box).

Heat 20 g / ²/3 oz / 4 tsp of butter and half the oil in a small pan over low heat and cook half of the onion until soft. Add half of the garlic and cook for 1 minute longer. Set aside to cool.

Heat the oven to 180°C / 350°F / gas 4.

Drain the apricots and cut into dice. Combine the apricots, onion and garlic mixture, and chopped spinach in a bowl and season.

Fill the pocket in each rabbit thigh with the spinach mixture, packing it in loosely. Sew up the opening with string or close with skewers. Heat a roasting pan on top of the stove and add the remaining oil. Arrange the rabbit portions in the pan and transfer to oven. Roast for 20–25 minutes.

Pick the tarragon leaves from the stalks;

set aside. Crush the peppercorns using the base of a heavy pan.

Remove the rabbit portions from the pan and set aside in a warm place. Pour all the fat from the pan. Put the pan over low heat on top of the stove and add 20 g / ²/3 oz / 4 tsp of the remaining butter. Cook the rest of the onions until soft, stirring often. Add the remaining garlic and cook for 1 minute longer. Stir in the white wine and peppercorns, increase the heat and bring to the boil. Add the tarragon stalks and boil until the wine has reduced by three-quarters.

Stir in the chicken concentrate, cream and horseradish and bring back to the boil. Simmer until the sauce thickens. Strain through a fine sieve, pressing on the vegetables and seasonings to extract flavour and liquid. Chop the tarragon and stir it into the sauce. Adjust the seasoning. Keep warm.

Heat the remaining butter and add the spinach leaves. Toss until heated through. Season with nutmeg, salt and pepper.

Remove the string or skewers from the rabbit and quarter each stuffed portion. Arrange on warmed plates with the spinach and pour the sauce over the rabbit. Serve with sauté potatoes.

TO BONE RABBIT LEG
To part bone each rabbit leg portion, working in from the thigh end, loosen the meat from around the thigh bone, pushing the meat back as you go. When you reach the joint between the thigh and drumstick, cut through it, taking care not to cut through the meat. Remove the thigh bone; the drumstick bone will remain. You will thus have a pocket in the thigh to stuff.

BOUDIN NOIR ON ONION MARMALADE WITH OLIVE OIL POTATOES

Serves 4

Individual French boudin noir, a type of black pudding [US blood sausage] with a delightful aniseed flavour, can be prepared by simply warming them in water. You could also use an English or American black pudding that you have to slice and grill, or even the spicy mergez sausage from North Africa.

4 French boudin noir, each weighing about
  120 g / 4 oz
2 celery stalks
4 oranges
4 handfuls of lamb's lettuce (mâche)
Olive Oil Potatoes (see page 141)
2 tbsp chopped fresh chives
1 tbsp Sherry Vinaigrette (see page 21)
salt and freshly ground black pepper

For the onion marmalade
600 g / 1 1/4 lb onions
15 g / 1/2 oz / 1 tbsp unsalted butter
4 tbsp groundnut oil [US peanut oil]
100 ml / 3 1/2 fl oz / 7 tbsp dry white wine
100 ml / 3 1/2 fl oz / 7 tbsp white wine
  vinegar
1 tbsp honey

First make the onion marmalade. Peel and thinly slice the onions. Heat the butter and oil in a large heavy-based frying pan over low heat. Add the onions, cover the pan and cook gently for 35–40 minutes or until they are very soft but not coloured, stirring often. Add the wine and vinegar and bring to the boil. Boil, uncovered, until completely evaporated. Stir in the honey and season with salt and pepper. Remove from the heat and set aside in a warm place.

Gently warm the boudin noir in a pan of simmering salted water for 8–10 minutes.

Meanwhile, peel the strings from the celery using a vegetable peeler and cut the stalks into fine slivers about 5 cm / 2 inches long. Peel the orange and cut out the segments (see page 72). Pick apart the lamb's lettuce, wash and dry. Mix the warm olive oil potatoes with the chives.

Spoon the onion marmalade on to the warmed plates and top with the boudin noir. Spoon the olive oil potatoes next to this. Arrange the orange segments around the edge of separate side plates. Toss the celery and lamb's lettuce with the vinaigrette, season with salt and pepper, and pile in the centre of the orange ring. Serve immediately.

FILLET STEAK WITH PESTO AND MEDITERRANEAN VEGETABLE RAGOÛT

Serves 4

Here, a good piece of beef is transformed into a really exciting delicacy.

*4 fillet steaks [US filet mignons], each
  weighing about 140 g / 5 oz
salt and freshly ground black pepper
3 tbsp vegetable oil
4 large flat mushrooms
20 g / ⅔ oz / 4 tsp unsalted butter*

*4 tbsp Pesto Sauce (see page 24)
4 tsp freshly grated Parmesan cheese
Mediterranean Vegetable Ragoût
  (see page 144)
sprigs of fresh rosemary, to garnish*

Heat the grill [US broiler] and the grill pan with rack in place.

Season the steaks with salt and pepper and turn them in the oil to coat. Arrange them on the hot grill rack and grill until they are cooked according to taste, turning them over once.

Meanwhile, remove the stalks from the mushrooms. When the steaks have been turned over, season the mushrooms, turn them in oil and arrange them, curved side up, on the rack with the steaks. Grill until lightly browned.

Turn the mushrooms over and put one-quarter of the butter into each cap. Continue grilling until tender.

Put a mushroom, curved side down, on each steak. Spread pesto sauce on the mushrooms and sprinkle with the Parmesan. Return to the grill, close to the heat, for 10 seconds, just to brown the top lightly.

Divide the vegetable ragoût among warmed plates, arranging it in a ring in the centre. Set the steaks on top and give them a turn of the peppermill. Garnish with rosemary and serve.

TIP

You can also cook the steak and mushrooms on a cast-iron grill pan on top of the stove. Heat the pan thoroughly. If there is not enough room to cook steaks and mushrooms at the same time, cook the steaks first and keep them warm while you cook the mushrooms.

RIGHT
*Fillet Steak with Pesto
and Mediterranean
Vegetable Ragoût*

RICH FRENCH BEEF STEW

Serves 4

This is a wonderfully robust dish for the autumn or winter. It goes well with pasta, couscous (see recipe on page 151), polenta (see recipe on page 127) or a potato purée. The stew is best made with fresh ox cheek, if you can get it.

1 kg / 2¼ lb boneless beef such as brisket or
  chuck
150 g / 5 oz button mushrooms
2 onions
2 carrots
2 celery stalks
1 large leek, white and pale green parts only
3 garlic cloves
1 bottle of dry red wine
salt and freshly ground black pepper
flour for coating

100 ml / 3½ fl oz / 7 tbsp vegetable oil
30 g / 1 oz / 2 tbsp unsalted butter
100 g / 3½ oz / 6 tbsp tomato paste
500 ml / 16 fl oz / 2 cups Chicken Essence
  (see page 14)
3 sprigs of fresh thyme
1 bay leaf
Mixed Spring Vegetables (see page 146),
  such as button onions, carrots and turnips,
  to serve

TIP
After straining the sauce, if it seems too liquid, boil to reduce it until it thickens slightly.

Trim all fat and sinew from the beef, then cut it into large cubes, about 5 cm / 2 inches square. Trim the mushrooms and quarter them if they are large. Peel the onions and carrots and cut them into 1-cm / ½-inch slices. Trim the celery and cut into 1-cm / ½-inch pieces. Trim the leek, cut it lengthwise in half and wash well, then cut into 1-cm / ½-inch pieces. Peel the garlic cloves.

Combine all the prepared ingredients in a large bowl and add the wine. Cover and leave to marinate in the refrigerator for 2 days.

Drain the meat and vegetables in a colander set in a bowl. Set the marinating liquid aside. Separate the beef and mushrooms from the other ingredients. Set the mushrooms aside.

Heat the oven to 150°C / 300°F / gas 2.

Pat the cubes of beef dry with paper towels. Season the cubes with salt and pepper, then dredge them with flour to coat lightly all over. Shake off excess flour. Heat a wide flameproof casserole over high heat and add enough oil to make a film on the bottom. Fry the cubes of beef, a few at a time, until well browned on all sides.

When all the beef has been browned and removed from the casserole, pour off the fat. Add a little more oil to the casserole with half of the butter and reduce the heat to moderate. Cook the marinated vegetables and garlic until soft and lightly browned, stirring often.

Stir in the tomato paste. Add a ladleful of the marinating liquid and bring to the boil. Boil until reduced to a glaze. Add another ladleful of the marinating liquid and boil to reduce again. Continue adding the liquid little by little, reducing it before adding the next batch.

When all the liquid has been added and reduced, stir in the chicken essence and bring to the boil. Return the beef to the casserole and add the herbs. Cover and transfer to the oven. Cook for 2½–3 hours or until the beef is very tender. Stir frequently.

Remove the cubes of beef with a slotted spoon. Strain the sauce through a fine sieve, pressing down on the vegetables to extract the maximum flavour and liquid. Taste and adjust the seasoning. Mix the beef back into the sauce and keep hot.

Heat a small frying pan over moderately high heat and add the remaining butter. Sauté the marinated mushrooms until they are tender. Season with salt and pepper.

Serve the beef stew in warmed soup plates, garnished with the mushrooms and mixed spring vegetables.

MARINATED STEAK WITH HORSERADISH KETCHUP

Serves 4

1/2 onion
2 garlic cloves
1/2 fresh hot red chilli pepper
3 1/2 tbsp vegetable oil
1 tbsp soy sauce
1 tbsp white wine vinegar
1 tbsp sugar

juice of 1 lemon
4 rump or boneless sirloin steaks, each weighing about 140 g / 5 oz
100 ml / 3 1/2 fl oz / 7 tbsp tomato ketchup
5 tbsp freshly grated horseradish
salt and freshly ground black pepper

Peel and chop the onion and garlic. Chop the chilli (discard the seeds for a less hot flavour). Combine the onion, garlic, chilli, oil, soy sauce, vinegar, sugar and lemon juice in a food processor and work until smooth.

Arrange the steaks in one layer in a shallow dish and pour the chilli mixture over them. Cover and leave to marinate in the refrigerator for 2–3 hours, turning the steaks occasionally.

When ready to cook, heat a cast-iron grill pan, or the grill [US broiler] and grill pan with rack in place, or a charcoal fire.

Mix together the ketchup and horseradish.

Drain the steaks and pat dry with paper towels. Season with salt and pepper. Grill until cooked to your taste, turning once. Give the steaks a turn of the peppermill and serve with the horseradish ketchup.

DOUBLE VEAL CUTLET WITH CHINESE LEAVES

Serves 4

These 'cutlets' are roasted on the bone, in 2-rib pieces. A perfect accompaniment is spinach spätzle (see recipe on page 150).

1 best end of neck of veal [US veal rib roast]
    containing 4 rib bones (see tip)
salt and freshly ground black pepper
2 tbsp groundnut oil [US peanut oil]
45 g / 1½ oz / 3 tbsp unsalted butter
100 g / 3½ oz fresh wild mushrooms such as
    chanterelles or girolles
1 garlic clove

5 sprigs of fresh mint
½ head of Chinese leaves [US Napa cabbage]
    or Chinese cabbage
1 tbsp finely chopped shallots
200 ml / 7 fl oz / ⅞ cup dry white wine
200 ml / 7 fl oz / ⅞ cup Chicken Concentrate
    (see page 16)

Heat the oven to 180°C / 350°F / gas 4.

Season the veal with salt and pepper. Heat a heavy-based roasting pan on top of the stove and add the oil and one-third of the butter. Put the veal in the pan and turn to coat with the fat. Transfer the pan to the oven and roast for about 35 minutes, turning the cutlets a couple of times.

Meanwhile, trim and wash the wild mushrooms; dry well on paper towels. Peel the garlic and chop to a paste (see page 13). Pull the mint leaves from the stalks; reserve both leaves and stalks.

Wash and drain the Chinese leaves. Cut into 3-cm / 1¼-inch squares, then blanch in boiling salted water for 1–2 minutes or until just tender but still firm. Drain well and refresh in iced water. Set aside.

When the veal has finished cooking, cut the piece of meat neatly from the bones in each double cutlet. Set the meat aside in a warm place to rest for 15–20 minutes.

Meanwhile, pour the fat from the roasting pan and add half of the remaining butter. Set the pan over low heat on top of the stove and cook the shallots until soft and translucent, stirring often. Add the garlic and cook gently for 1 minute longer.

Add the wild mushrooms and season. Cook for 1–2 minutes, stirring. Remove with a slotted spoon and reserve.

Add the wine to the pan with the mint stalks. Bring to the boil, stirring well to mix in the browned bits on the pan base. Boil until reduced by two-thirds.

Add the chicken concentrate to the sauce and continue boiling until reduced by about one-quarter.

Strain the sauce through a fine sieve into a saucepan, pressing on the vegetables and flavourings to extract maximum flavour and liquid. Return the mushrooms to the sauce. Chop the mint leaves and stir into the sauce. Taste and adjust the seasoning. Keep warm.

Melt the remaining butter in a pan over moderate heat and toss the Chinese leaves until piping hot. Season with salt and pepper. Spoon the leaves on to warmed plates. Cut the veal into 5-mm / ¼-inch slices and arrange on the Chinese leaves. Serve the sauce on the side.

TIPS

Ask your butcher to remove the chine bone and to cut the piece of meat in half, so each half has 2 rib bones. When prepared, each 'double cutlet' should weigh about 450 g / 1 lb. Trim off any skin and most of the fat.

If you like, you can serve the cutlets whole, and carve them at the table. If you do this, slice the meat parallel to the bones, holding the ends of the bones to keep the cutlets steady.

VEAL STEAK WITH LEEKS AND ALMONDS

Serves 4

Serve with deep-fried potatoes filled with mixed spring vegetables (see recipes on pages 142 and 146).

Serve with deep-fried potatoes filled with mixed spring vegetables (see recipes on pages 142 and 146).

TIPS

If the leek sauce should separate when it is being reheated, just whisk in half a spoonful of cold double cream [US heavy whipping cream].

When crushing a large quantity of pepper- corns or other spice seeds or berries, cover the pan with a towel so that the peppercorns don't fly everywhere when you press on the pan to crush them. Alternatively, use a mortar and pestle.

225 g / 8 oz leeks, white and pale green parts only
45 g / 1 1/2 oz / 3 tbsp unsalted butter
salt and freshly ground black pepper
1 tsp white wine vinegar
100 ml / 3 1/2 fl oz / 7 tbsp dry white wine
200 ml / 7 fl oz / 7/8 cup Chicken Essence (see page 14)

2 ripe but firm plum tomatoes
1 egg
3 tbsp very finely chopped blanched almonds
2 tbsp chopped fresh parsley
3 tbsp black peppercorns
4 boneless veal steaks cut from the loin, each weighing about 140 g / 5 oz
100 ml / 3 1/2 fl oz / 7 tbsp olive oil

Trim the leeks, cut them in half lengthwise and wash thoroughly, then cut across into thin slices. Heat half the butter in a heavy-based pan over low heat. Add the leeks and season with salt and pepper. Cover the pan and cook gently for about 8 minutes or until the leeks are soft but not coloured. Stir often.

Remove 2 tbsp of the leeks and reserve. Add the vinegar and wine to the leeks in the pan and bring to the boil. Boil, uncovered, until almost completely evaporated. Stir in the chicken essence and boil until reduced by three-quarters.

Meanwhile, peel the tomatoes and remove the seeds (see page 74), then dice the flesh. Lightly beat the egg in a shallow dish. In another shallow dish combine the almonds and parsley. Crush the pepper-corns finely with the base of a small heavy pan and stir into the almonds and parsley.

Trim all fat from the veal steaks and sea-son them with salt and pepper. Turn them in the beaten egg, then coat all over with the almond mixture.

Heat a frying pan over moderate heat; add 1 tbsp of the olive oil and the remain-ing butter. Fry the veal steaks for about 6 minutes or until the coating is golden brown, turning once. The meat should be pink in the centre. Remove the veal steaks to a plate and keep warm.

When the leek sauce is sufficiently reduced, pour it into a blender or food processor and work until smooth. With the machine running, slowly add the remaining olive oil through the feed tube. Pour the sauce back into the pan and stir in the reserved leeks and the tomatoes. Reheat gently, stirring constant-ly; do not allow to boil. Taste and adjust the seasoning.

Place a veal steak in the centre of each warmed plate and pour the leek sauce around it. Give the veal a turn of the peppermill and serve immediately.

BRAISED VEAL KNUCKLE WITH POLENTA

Serves 4

Make this dish in the cold weather months – it is very comforting and filling. The sauce is absolutely gorgeous.

1 veal knuckle [US veal shank], weighing
  about 2 kg / 4¼ lb
salt and freshly ground black pepper
1 large onion
2 carrots
1 celery stalk
1 leek, white and pale green parts only
200 g / 7 oz ripe but firm plum tomatoes
2 garlic cloves
25 g / ¾ oz / 1½ tbsp unsalted butter
1½ tbsp groundnut oil [US peanut oil]
50 g / 1¾ oz / 3 tbsp tomato paste
250 ml / 8 fl oz / 1 cup dry white wine

500 ml / 16 fl oz / 2 cups Chicken
  Concentrate (see page 16)
½ tsp black peppercorns
1 sprig of fresh rosemary
1 sprig of fresh thyme
Polenta (see box), to serve

For the garnish
225 g / 8 oz mixed vegetables: French beans
  [US thin green beans], carrots, swede
  [US rutabaga] and kohlrabi
15 g / ½ oz / 1 tbsp unsalted butter

Ask your butcher to trim off the meat, skin and gristle from the top 5 cm / 2 inches of bone at the thin end of the knuckle. Trim the other end of the knuckle to tidy it up and season it with salt and pepper.

Peel the onion and carrots. Trim the celery. Cut the vegetables into small cubes. Trim the leek, cut it lengthwise in half and wash it well, then cut into small cubes. Peel the tomatoes and remove the seeds (see page 74); reserve the skins and seeds. Cut the tomato flesh into dice. Peel the garlic cloves and cut them in half.

Heat a flameproof casserole just large enough to hold the knuckle comfortably. Add the butter and oil, then add the knuckle and brown it on all sides over moderate heat. Remove it from the pot.

Heat the oven to 180°C / 350°F / gas 4.

Add the onion, garlic, carrots, celery and leek to the casserole and cook until soft and lightly browned, stirring constantly. Stir in the tomato paste and the reserved tomato skins and seeds. Cook for 1 minute, stirring.

Stir a little of the wine into the vegetable mixture and boil until evaporated. Stir in the remaining wine little by little and boil to evaporate, stirring frequently.

Return the veal knuckle to the casserole and add half the chicken concentrate.

Lightly crush the peppercorns with the base of a small pan and add to the casserole with the herbs. Cover and transfer to the oven. Braise for about 3 hours or until the meat is very tender and is falling off the bone. Turn the knuckle frequently and add the remaining chicken concentrate little by little as it evaporates. Remove the lid for the last 20 minutes of cooking so the knuckle will have a good colour. (Be careful to check often after this because the liquid will evaporate more quickly. If necessary, add a little water.)

About 20 minutes before the veal has finished cooking, prepare the vegetables for

OVER PAGE
*Braised Veal Knuckle
with Polenta*

> **TIPS**
> By adding the wine gradually, the sugar in the tomato skins and seeds and in the tomato paste can reduce and caramelize. This will give a rich colour and shine to the finished sauce.
>
> Do not discard the knuckle bone. Dry it and then extract the bone marrow. Perhaps you could add it to your next batch of chicken essence.

garnish. Trim or peel them as necessary, then cut into thin sticks about 10 cm / 4 inches long or the same size as the beans. Cook them in separate pans of boiling salted water until just tender. Drain and refresh in iced water, then drain again and set aside.

Remove the knuckle from the casserole and keep it warm. Strain the sauce through a fine sieve into a saucepan, pressing on the vegetables and seasonings to extract the maximum flavour and liquid. Bring to the boil, then stir in the diced tomato. Taste and adjust the seasoning. Keep warm.

Take the meat from the knuckle bone (it should come off very easily in one piece). Cut it across into 5-mm / ¼-inch slices.

Divide the hot polenta among large warmed soup plates. Arrange the meat on top and spoon over the sauce. Keep warm. Toss the garnish vegetables in hot butter to reheat them, then season with salt and pepper. Place the buttered vegetables on top of the sauce and serve.

POLENTA

Put 500 ml / 16 fl oz / 2 cups of Chicken Essence (see page 14) in a saucepan and bring to the boil. Whisk in 150 g / 5 oz / 1 cup + 2½ tbsp polenta or cornmeal in a thin steady stream. Cook for 4–6 minutes or until thick, whisking constantly. Whisk in 30 g / 1 oz / 2 tbsp unsalted butter and season to taste with grated nutmeg, salt and pepper. Pour into a shallow pan, about 24 x 30 cm / 9½ x 12 inches, to make a layer about 2-cm / ¾-inch thick. Leave to cool. When the polenta is cold and set, cut it into 6-cm / 2½-inch long diamond shapes. Before serving, fry in hot olive oil or unsalted butter until golden brown on both sides.

SHOULDER OF LAMB WITH GOAT'S CHEESE STUFFING AND SPICY HERB CRUST

Serves 6-8

Goat's cheese and basil give this stuffing a soft and mellow flavour that combines perfectly with juicy, tender lamb. The spicy crust is the perfect finishing touch. The crust could also be used on roast pork or veal.

1 shoulder of lamb, weighing about 2 kg /
*   4 1/2 lb*
salt and freshly ground black pepper
4 tbsp groundnut oil [US peanut oil]
2 ripe but firm plum tomatoes
100 ml / 3 1/2 fl oz / 7 tbsp dry white wine
250 ml / 8 fl oz / 1 cup Chicken Concentrate
*   (see page 16)*
1 sprig of fresh rosemary
Spicy Herb Crust (see box)

For the goat's cheese stuffing
3 onions
2 garlic cloves
6 sprigs of fresh basil
6 sprigs of fresh coriander [US cilantro]
120 g / 4 oz firm goat's cheese
15 g / 1/2 oz / 1 tbsp unsalted butter
1 tbsp groundnut oil [US peanut oil]
150 g / 5 oz minced [US ground] lamb or
*   pork, or a mixture of half lamb and*
*   half pork*
4 tbsp chopped fresh flat-leaf (Italian) parsley
1 egg
1 egg yolk
3 tbsp double cream [US heavy whipping
*   cream]*
freshly grated nutmeg

Ask your butcher to bone the lamb shoulder without cutting up the meat.

To make the stuffing, peel and finely chop the onions. Peel the garlic and chop to a paste (see page 13). Pull the basil and coriander leaves from the stalks and reserve both stalks and leaves. Cut the goat's cheese into 1-cm / 1/2-inch cubes. Heat the butter and oil in a frying pan over low heat and cook half of the onion until soft and translucent, stirring often. Add half of the garlic and cook gently for 1 minute longer. Remove from the heat and leave to cool.

Put the lamb or pork in a bowl. Chop the basil and coriander leaves and add to the meat with the parsley and softened onion and garlic. Mix well. Beat in the egg and egg yolk. Then beat in the cream. Season with nutmeg, salt and pepper. Mix in the cubes of goat's cheese.

Heat the oven to 200°C / 400°F / gas 6.

Season the cavities in the shoulder of lamb, then fill loosely with the stuffing. Sew up the openings or close them securely with skewers. Season the outside with salt and pepper.

Heat a roasting pan on top of the stove. Add 3 tbsp of the oil, then put the shoulder of lamb in the pan and turn to coat it with oil. Transfer the pan to the oven and roast for about 20 minutes. Turn down the oven temperature to 180°C / 350°F / gas 4 and continue roasting for 1 hour 10 minutes or until the lamb is cooked to your liking (test with a skewer: the juices that run out should be slightly pink). During roasting, turn the shoulder and baste it frequently with the fat in the pan.

About 30 minutes before the lamb has

TIPS

It is a good idea to take a spoonful of the stuffing and to fry it in a little oil so that you can check the seasoning. Then, if necessary, you can add more salt and pepper to the rest of the stuffing.

For a delicious and unusual hamburger, make up the stuffing mixture with half pork and half beef, shape it, and fry in oil and butter.

If more convenient, you can colour the spicy crust under a hot grill [US broiler].

finished roasting, add the remaining chopped onions to the pan.

Meanwhile, roughly chop the tomatoes and make the spicy herb crust.

When the lamb is ready, remove it from the oven and transfer it from the pan to a plate. Set aside in a warm place to rest for at least 20 minutes. Increase the oven temperature to 230°C / 450°F / gas 8.

Spoon as much of the fat as possible from the roasting pan, reserving the onions and any juices from the lamb. Add the remaining oil and the remaining garlic to the onions and fry over moderately high heat until slightly caramelized, stirring constantly. Add the basil and coriander stalks, tomatoes and wine and bring to the boil, stirring well. Boil until reduced by half.

Add the chicken concentrate and rosemary. Bring back to the boil and boil for 5 minutes.

Remove and discard the rosemary. Purée the sauce in a blender or food processor, then strain it through a fine sieve into a saucepan, pressing on the vegetables and herbs to extract the maximum liquid and flavour. Taste and adjust the seasoning and keep warm.

Remove the string or skewers from the lamb and set it in a roasting pan or on a baking sheet. (Add any juices from the lamb to the sauce.) Spread the spicy herb crust over the top in a 5-mm / 1/4-inch thick layer. Roast for about 10 minutes to crisp the crust.

Carve the lamb and serve with the sauce.

SPICY HERB CRUST

Remove the core and seeds from 2 small sweet peppers (1 red and 1 green), then cut into very fine dice. Peel 2 garlic cloves and chop to a paste (see page 13). Finely chop 1 hot red chilli pepper, removing the seeds first if you prefer a less hot flavour. Heat 1 tbsp olive oil in a frying pan over low heat and cook the pepper dice, covered, until tender but still firm, stirring often. Add the garlic and chilli pepper and cook gently for 1 minute longer. Remove from the heat and add 130 g / 4 1/2 oz / 2 3/4 cups fine fresh white breadcrumbs, 60 g /2 oz / 4 tbsp softened unsalted butter and 60 g / 2 oz / 1 cup chopped mixed fresh rosemary and parsley. Mix well and season with salt and pepper.

NAVARIN OF LAMB WITH COUSCOUS AND GRILLED VEGETABLES

Serves 4

A very succulent dish, with an intense flavour of herbs. A good Navarin divides the serious cook from the part-timer. If you prefer, you can serve a selection of baby vegetables (see page 146) rather than grilled vegetables.

TIP

Prepare the grilled vegetables and couscous while the lamb is braising.

8 pieces of lamb from the middle neck [US lamb shoulder blade chops], 4–5 cm / 1¹/₂–2 inches thick, each weighing about 90 g / 3 oz
1 large onion
1 carrot
5 garlic cloves
1 leek, white and pale green parts only
salt and freshly ground black pepper
3 tbsp groundnut oil [US peanut oil]
50 g / 1³/₄ oz / 3 tbsp tomato paste

300 ml / ¹/₂ pint / 1¹/₄ cups red wine
20 g / ²/₃ oz / 2 tbsp flour
750 ml / 1¹/₄ pints / 3 cups Chicken Essence (see page 14)
1 sprig of fresh thyme
1 sprig of fresh marjoram

For serving
Grilled Vegetables (see page 145)
Sophie's Couscous (see page 151)

Heat the oven to 180°C / 350°F / gas 4.

Trim the pieces of lamb. Peel and roughly chop the onion, carrot and garlic. Trim the leek, cut lengthwise in half and wash thoroughly, then chop it.

Season the lamb with salt and pepper. Heat a flameproof casserole over high heat and add the oil. Brown the pieces of lamb briskly on both sides. Remove and set aside. Add the prepared vegetables to the casserole and cook over moderately low heat until lightly browned, stirring often.

Add the tomato paste and cook for 30 seconds, stirring well. Add one-third of the wine, stir well and bring to the boil. Boil until reduced to a thick glaze. Repeat with the remaining wine, adding it in 2 batches.

Add the flour and stir well for 1 minute, then gradually stir in the cold chicken essence. Bring to the boil. Add the herbs and some salt and pepper, then return the lamb to the casserole. Cover and transfer to the oven. Braise for about 2 hours or until the lamb is very tender, stirring occasionally.

Remove the pieces of lamb from the casserole and keep warm. Strain the sauce through a fine sieve, pressing down on the vegetables and seasonings to extract the maximum flavour and liquid, and taste and adjust the seasoning. Spoon the sauce over the lamb and serve with the grilled vegetables and couscous on the side.

RIGHT
Navarin of Lamb with Couscous and Grilled Vegetables

GRILLED LAMB CUTLETS WITH A POTATO-MINT CRUST

Serves 4

225 g / 8 oz potatoes
1/2 onion
1 large garlic clove
1/2 fresh hot red chilli pepper
about 5 tbsp vegetable oil
10 sprigs of fresh mint
6 black olives
1 1/2 tbsp freshly grated Parmesan cheese

2 tbsp extra virgin olive oil
1 egg yolk
salt and freshly ground black pepper
4 baby aubergines [US eggplants]
8 cherry tomatoes
8 lamb cutlets [US lamb rib chops], each
    weighing about 75 g / 2 1/2 oz

Peel the potatoes, then cook them in boiling salted water for 15-20 minutes or until tender.

Peel and finely chop the onion. Peel the garlic and chop to a paste (see page 13). Finely chop the chilli pepper (discard the seeds if you want a less hot flavour). Heat 2 tbsp of the vegetable oil in a small pan over low heat and cook the onion until soft and translucent, stirring often. Add the garlic and cook gently for 1 minute longer. Add the chilli and cook for a further minute. Remove from the heat.

Drain the potatoes in a colander, then return them to the pan and dry out over low heat. Press the potatoes through a fine sieve or potato ricer into a bowl.

Add the softened vegetables to the potato purée. Finely chop the mint leaves and add to the potato mixture. Remove the stones [US pits] from the olives and chop finely, then add to the potato mixture together with the Parmesan, 1 tbsp of the olive oil and the egg yolk. Season with salt and pepper and mix well. Keep warm.

Heat the grill [US broiler] and the grill pan with rack in place. Heat the oven to 200°C / 400°F / gas 6.

Score a cross in the base of each aubergine, then turn in vegetable oil to coat all sides. Grill for 8–10 minutes or until the skin is lightly charred and wrinkled all over and the flesh is tender (test it with a skewer or knife).

Meanwhile, peel the cherry tomatoes (see page 74) and cut them into 5-mm / 1/4-inch slices.

Peel the aubergines and cut each lengthwise in half. Slice each half thinly, lengthwise, not cutting through at one end, then fan out the slices slightly. Place the aubergine fans in a lightly oiled baking pan and arrange the tomato slices in the fanned aubergine slices. Set aside.

Season the lamb cutlets and arrange on the hot grill rack. Grill until almost cooked to your liking, turning once. Spread the potato mixture on each cutlet in a 1-cm / 1/2-inch layer. Grill for about 2 minutes longer or until the crust is slightly crisp and lightly browned.

Meanwhile, season the aubergine fans and tomatoes with salt and pepper and brush with the remaining olive oil. Heat in the oven for 5 minutes.

Arrange the lamb cutlets with the aubergine and tomato fans on warmed plates and serve immediately.

CALF'S LIVER WITH APPLE AND ONION RINGS

Serves 4

In Germany, this dish is known as 'Himmel und Erde' (Heaven and Earth). Olive oil potatoes (see recipe on page 141) are a perfect accompaniment for the liver.

1 large onion
2 apples
vegetable oil for frying
30 g / 1 oz / 2 tbsp unsalted butter
8 slices of calf's liver, each weighing about
  60 g / 2 oz
salt and freshly ground black pepper

100 ml / 3 1/2 fl oz / 7 tbsp dry white wine
200 ml / 7 fl oz / 7/8 cup Chicken Concentrate
  (see page 16)
50 g / 3/4 oz / 1/3 cup flour
1/2 tsp paprika
a little milk
4 fresh sage leaves

Peel the onion and cut it into 3-mm / 1/8-inch slices. Separate into rings and discard the small central rings.

Peel the apples and remove the cores with an apple corer. Cut each apple across into equal-size rings that are 5 mm / 1/4 inch thick. Discard the smaller ends.

Heat a pan of oil for deep frying to 180°C / 350°F.

Meanwhile, heat a heavy-based frying pan over moderate heat and add half the butter and 1 tbsp oil. Fry the apple rings until they are golden brown and tender, turning so that they cook evenly. Remove the apple rings with a palette knife [US metal spatula] and keep hot.

Pour the fat from the pan and add the remaining butter and another 1 tbsp oil. Fry the slices of liver until browned on both sides. They should be medium rare in

the centre. Remove them from the pan and season with salt and pepper. Keep hot.

Pour the wine into the pan and bring to the boil, stirring to mix in all the browned bits from the bottom. Boil until reduced by half. Stir in the chicken concentrate and bring back to the boil. Simmer until slightly thickened.

Meanwhile, mix the flour and paprika on a plate. Dip the onion rings in milk, then coat in the flour, shaking off any excess. Deep fry in the hot oil until golden brown on all sides. Drain on paper towels and keep hot.

Cut the sage leaves into fine strips. Add the sage to the sauce, and taste and adjust the seasoning.

Place the slices of liver on warmed plates and garnish with onion and apple rings. Pour the sauce around and serve.

PAUPIETTES OF PORK WITH SAGE AND ONION STUFFING

Serves 4

8 thin slices of pork from the centre of the
  fillet [US tenderloin], each weighing
  about 60 g / 2 oz
8 thin slices of streaky bacon [US Canadian
  bacon]
2 tsp Dijon mustard
4 tbsp groundnut oil [US peanut oil]
45 g / 1¹/₂ oz / 3 tbsp unsalted butter
4 tbsp dry white wine
100 ml / 3¹/₂ fl oz / 7 tbsp Chicken
  Concentrate (see page 16)
salt and freshly ground black pepper

For the stuffing
1 small onion
1 small garlic clove
45 g / 1¹/₂ oz / 3 tbsp unsalted butter
2 tbsp groundnut oil [US peanut oil]
90 g / 3 oz / 2 cups fine fresh white
  breadcrumbs
4 tbsp chopped fresh parsley
2 tbsp chopped fresh sage
finely grated zest of 1 small unwaxed lemon
finely grated zest of 1 small unwaxed orange

TIPS

Under no circum-
stances must the pork
be overcooked or it
will lose its flavour
and juiciness.

These can be served
with polenta (see
recipe on page 127).

First make the stuffing. Peel and finely chop the onion. Peel the garlic and chop to a paste (see page 13). Heat the butter and oil in a small pan over low heat and cook the onion until soft and translucent, stirring often. Add the garlic and cook for 1 minute longer. Remove from the heat.

Add the breadcrumbs and mix well with the onion and garlic. Mix in the herbs and zests and season with salt and pepper.

Heat the oven to 190°C / 375°F / gas 5.

Trim any fat from the slices of pork. Put them between sheets of cling film [US plastic wrap] and pound gently until they are about 3 mm / ¹/₈ inch thick. Trim the edges to neaten them. Each slice should measure about 12.5 cm / 5 inches square. Trim any rind from the bacon, then stretch each slice by smoothing it out with the blunt side of a knife.

Brush each slice of pork thinly with mustard. Divide the stuffing among the pork slices, spreading it out evenly. Roll up each slice of pork and wrap a piece of bacon diagonally around it. Secure with wooden cocktail sticks.

Heat a heavy-based roasting pan on top of the stove. Add the oil and one-third of the butter. Place the pork paupiettes in the pan and cook over moderately high heat to brown them on all sides. Cover the paupiettes with a buttered paper or foil and transfer the pan to the oven. Cook for about 10 minutes, turning the paupiettes once or twice.

Remove the paupiettes from the pan and keep them warm. Pour off the fat from the pan, then add the wine. Set the pan over moderately high heat and bring to the boil, stirring well to mix in any browned bits. Boil until the wine has reduced by two-thirds. Stir in the chicken concentrate and bring back to the boil. Cut the remaining butter into small pieces and add a few at a time, swirling the sauce to melt and incorporate the butter. Taste and adjust the seasoning.

Remove the sticks from the paupiettes, give them a turn of the peppermill and serve with the sauce.

PORK FILLET WITH FENNEL AND CARAWAY SAUCE

Serves 4

2 whole pork fillets [US pork tenderloins],
 each weighing about 300 g/10 oz
45 g / 1 1/2oz / 3 tbsp unsalted butter
3 tbsp groundnut oil [US peanut oil]
salt and freshly ground black pepper
1 large onion
1 garlic clove
100 ml /3 1/2 fl oz / 7 tbsp port wine
1 tsp black peppercorns

1 tbsp caraway seeds
300 ml / 1/2 pint / 1 1/4 cups Chicken
 Concentrate (see page 16)

For the fennel gratin
2 fennel bulbs, each weighing about
 200 g / 7 oz
2 ripe but firm plum tomatoes
50 g / 1 3/4 oz Emmenthal cheese

TIPS
You might like to try
this with spinach
spätzle (see recipe on
page 150).

Caraway seeds vary
greatly in strength –
the fresher they are,
the more intense the
flavour will be. Do not
be afraid to use them
generously because
the flavour is
wonderful.

The caraway sauce
would also go very
well with beef.

Heat the oven to 220°C / 425°F / gas 7.

First prepare the fennel. Trim the tops from the bulbs, then cook them in boiling salted water for 10–15 minutes or until they are tender. Drain, refresh in cold water, drain again and set aside. Peel the tomatoes and remove the seeds (see page 74). Cut the tomato flesh neatly into small dice. Grate the cheese.

Trim all skin and fat from the pork. Heat one-third of the butter and 2 tbsp oil in a flameproof casserole in the oven. Season the pork, add it to the casserole and turn to coat with the fat. Roast for about 10 minutes.

Meanwhile, peel and finely chop the onion. Peel the garlic and chop to a paste (see page 13).

Remove the pork to a plate, cover with foil and return it to the turned-off oven to keep warm. Pour away all of the fat from the casserole and set it over low heat on top of the stove. Add half of the remaining butter and the rest of the oil. Cook the onion until soft and translucent, stirring often. Add the garlic and cook gently for 1 minute longer. Stir in the port and bring to the boil. Boil until reduced by half.

Cut each fennel bulb lengthwise into four 1-cm / 1/2-inch slices. Arrange in one layer on a baking tray. Season the fennel slices with salt and pepper and cover with the tomato dice. Put into the turned-off oven to warm.

Coarsely crush the peppercorns with the base of a small heavy pan and add to the casserole. Put the remaining butter and a little salt on a chopping board and add the caraway seeds. Chop the seeds well into the butter. Add the caraway butter to the casserole with the chicken concentrate. Simmer the sauce for about 10 minutes or until reduced by one-third.

Meanwhile, heat the grill [US broiler]. Sprinkle the tomato-topped fennel slices with the cheese. Grill until the cheese has melted and is golden brown.

Strain the sauce through a fine sieve into a saucepan, pressing on the vegetables and seasonings to extract the flavour and liquid. Adjust the seasoning. Reheat gently.

Divide the fennel among the warmed plates, arranging it in the middle. Cut the pork at an angle into 1-cm / 1/2-inch slices and arrange around the fennel. Pour the sauce over the pork and serve.

NOISETTES OF VENISON ON CELERIAC PURÉE

Serves 4

Celeriac is a little-used vegetable that deserves to be eaten a lot more often. It goes well with all game and with duck, and is best in the autumn and winter.

juice of 1/2 lemon
1 celeriac [US celery root], weighing about
 900 g / 2 lb
60 g / 2 oz / 4 tbsp unsalted butter
2 tsp crème fraîche or double cream
 [US heavy whipping cream]
salt and freshly ground black pepper
2 shallots
1 garlic clove

4 noisettes of venison, cut from the saddle,
 about 1.5-cm / 3/4-inch thick, each
 weighing about 120 g / 4 oz
2 tbsp groundnut oil [US peanut oil]
4 tbsp dry red wine
1/2 tsp cardamom seeds removed from the pods
200 ml / 7 fl oz / 7/8 cup Chicken Concentrate
 (see page 16)
Mushroom-filled Pastry Leaves
 (see page 152), to garnish (optional)

Bring a saucepan of salted water to the boil and add the lemon juice. Peel the celeriac and cut it into 1-cm / 1/2-inch cubes. Drop immediately into the pan of boiling salted water, cover and simmer for about 20 minutes or until very tender.

Drain well, then purée the celeriac in a food processor. If it is at all stringy, press it through a fine sieve. Return it to the saucepan and dry out a little over low heat if necessary, stirring constantly. Add one-half of the butter and the cream and season with salt and pepper. Set aside.

Peel and finely chop the shallots. Peel the garlic and chop to a paste (see page 13).

Season the noisettes with salt and pepper. Heat a heavy-based frying pan over moderately high heat and add half the remaining butter and half the oil. Put the noisettes in the pan and fry until browned on both sides and cooked to your taste: 6 minutes cooking will produce medium to medium rare meat. Remove the noisettes from the pan and keep them warm.

Pour the fat from the pan and add the remaining butter and oil. Heat over low heat, then add the shallots and cook until soft and translucent, stirring often. Add the garlic and cook for 1 minute longer. Stir in the red wine, bring to the boil and boil until reduced by half.

Coarsely crush the cardamom seeds with the side of a knife. Add to the pan with the chicken concentrate. Bring back to the boil and boil for 2 minutes or until slightly thickened.

Meanwhile, reheat the celeriac purée.

Strain the sauce through a fine sieve, pressing on the vegetables and seasonings to extract maximum flavour and liquid, and taste and adjust the seasoning.

Spoon the celeriac purée on to the warmed plates and press in the noisettes. Pour the sauce over and around. Give the noisettes a turn of the peppermill, garnish with the mushroom-filled pastry leaves, if using, and serve.

GARNISHES AND ACCOMPANIMENTS

COOKING vegetables takes as much skill and devotion as cooking fish or meat. There is nothing worse than over-cooked vegetables, but under-cooked vegetables are almost as bad. The point at which a vegetable changes from raw to *al dente* (just tender to the bite) needs careful judgement.

The ground rule here is that green vegetables should be cooked *al dente*, with the exception of Brussels sprouts which are inedible if only half-cooked. Root vegetables should be well cooked, as their flavour, texture and colour are brought out then.

Vegetables must always be at their freshest. Do not keep them in a warm place or, indeed, for too long in the refrigerator as they will lose colour and flavour, as well as many nutrients. Treat them with care: one of the greatest delights in cooking is to watch the transformation of a vegetable from raw to cooked, retaining all its colour and flavour, and turning it into an absolute delicacy. This is what vegetables should be every time, whether served to accompany a main dish or to be enjoyed on their own.

SAUTÉ POTATOES

Serves 4

600 g / 1 1/4 lb medium-sized new potatoes
salt and freshly ground black pepper
1/2 tsp caraway seeds
2 garlic cloves

4 tbsp groundnut oil [US peanut oil]
60 g / 2 oz / 4 tbsp unsalted butter
3 sprigs of fresh rosemary

Wash the potatoes, then put them in a saucepan. Cover with cold water and add some salt and the caraway seeds. Bring to the boil and simmer for 12–15 minutes or until the potatoes are nearly tender. Drain.

When the potatoes are cool enough to handle, peel them (or leave skins on if you prefer). Cut the potatoes into 5-mm / 1/4-inch slices. Peel and slice the garlic.

Heat a large frying pan over a moderate heat and add 3 tbsp of the oil. Add the potatoes, spreading them out in the pan. Add the garlic, 45 g / 1 1/2 oz / 3 tbsp of the

butter and 2 sprigs of rosemary. Fry until the potato slices are golden brown on both sides, turning constantly and carefully so that they colour and cook evenly. Season with salt and pepper.

Drain the potatoes on paper towels. Discard the rosemary sprigs, if you like. Put the potatoes in a warmed serving dish.

Heat the remaining oil and butter in the pan. Pull the rosemary leaves from the remaining sprig and add them to the pan. Toss briefly until fragrant, then scatter over the potatoes. Serve immediately.

TIPS

It is better to cook and peel the potatoes the day before you fry them because they will be very firm then and will not fall apart easily.

If more convenient, you can fry the potatoes and keep them warm in a low oven for 15–20 minutes. Don't cover them or they'll become soggy.

POTATO RATATOUILLE

Serves 4

1 carrot, weighing about 120 g / 4 oz
1/4 celeriac [US celery root], weighing about 90 g / 3 oz
1 potato, weighing about 200 g / 7 oz
2 medium-sized celery stalks
1 medium-sized courgette [US zucchini], weighing about 120 g / 4 oz

3 tbsp olive oil
3 tbsp dry white wine
125 ml / 4 fl oz / 1/2 cup Chicken Essence (see page 14)
2 tbsp chopped fresh coriander [US cilantro]
salt and freshly ground black pepper

Peel the carrot, celeriac and potato. Trim the celery and courgette. Cut all the vegetables into small, neat cubes. Heat 2 tbsp oil in a frying pan over low heat and cook the carrot, celeriac and potato for 2 minutes, stirring occasionally.

Stir in the wine and boil until reduced to a glaze. Stir in half the chicken essence.

Add the celery and cook for 5 minutes, then stir in the courgette. Continue cooking, gradually adding the remaining essence and stirring, until all the vegetables are just tender and the essence has evaporated.

Stir in the remaining olive oil and the coriander and season. Serve hot.

TIPS

Ideally, equal prepared weights of each vegetable should be used to make this dish, and they should all be cut into dice of the same size.

Fresh herbs should always be chopped at the last minute, just before using, because they quickly lose their pungent flavour.

WARM POTATO SALAD

Serves 4

600 g / 1 1/4 lb new potatoes
1 tsp caraway seeds
salt and freshly ground black pepper
1 small onion
1 small garlic clove

3-cm / 1 1/4-inch piece of cucumber
2 ripe but firm plum tomatoes
4 tbsp Chicken Concentrate (see page 16)
2 tbsp white wine vinegar
4 tbsp chopped fresh chives

TIPS

According to the time of year and the type of potato you use, they may absorb more liquid. So you may have to add more chicken concentrate and vinegar.

If using very new potatoes there is no need to peel them.

This salad goes very well with pork, chicken and deep-fried fish.

Scrub the potatoes but do not peel them. Put them in a saucepan of cold water, add the caraway seeds and some salt, and bring to the boil. Simmer for about 15 minutes or until just tender.

Peel and finely chop the onion. Peel the garlic and chop to a paste (see page 13). Peel the piece of cucumber, cut it in half lengthwise and scoop out the seeds with a teaspoon. Cut the halves across into fine slices. Cut out the tomato stalks, then cut the tomatoes into thin wedges.

Drain the potatoes and rinse briefly under cold running water. When they are cool enough to handle, peel them and cut into 5-mm / 1/4-inch slices.

Combine the potatoes, onion, cucumber and tomato in a bowl. Warm the chicken essence and stir in the garlic and vinegar. Add to the vegetables. Season. Mix together gently, then set aside in a warm place for about 10 minutes so the potatoes can soak up the dressing. Adjust the seasoning, sprinkle with the chives and serve.

OLIVE OIL POTATOES

Serves 4

Once you have tried these potatoes, you will never want to eat ordinary mashed potatoes again.

700 g / 1 1/2 lb potatoes
150 ml / 1/4 pint / 2/3 cup olive oil, preferably extra virgin
45 g / 1 1/2 oz garlic cloves, about 18 medium-sized

salt and freshly ground black pepper
4 tbsp milk
5 tbsp double cream [US heavy whipping cream]

TIPS

If the potatoes show any signs of separating when you are adding the heated milk and oil mixture, just add a little extra cold cream.

A small spoonful of truffle oil adds a nice twist to the potatoes.

Serve with poultry, fish or meat.

Peel the potatoes and cut into large cubes. Place in a saucepan, just cover with cold water and add one-third of the oil, the peeled garlic cloves and salt. Bring to the boil and simmer for 15–20 minutes or until the potatoes are tender but not mushy.

Drain well. Transfer the garlic to a board and crush with the side of a knife. Heat 1 tbsp olive oil in a frying pan over moder-

ately low heat and cook the garlic for 1 minute. Do not allow it to colour.

Return the garlic to the potatoes and press through a fine sieve into a bowl. Or use a potato ricer or masher.

Heat the milk, cream and remaining oil in a saucepan. Gradually add to the potatoes, mixing well with a wooden spoon. Season with salt and pepper, and serve.

DEEP-FRIED POTATOES

Serves 4

Fill these potatoes with mixed spring vegetables (see recipe on page 146), or with a ragoût of courgettes [US zucchini] and tomatoes glazed with cheese, or with creamed wild mushrooms (see page 152).

*4 firm, boiling potatoes, each weighing about
    200 g / 7 oz
salt and freshly ground black pepper
vegetable oil for deep frying*

*1 egg
flour for dusting
45 g / 1¹/₂ oz / 1 cup fine fresh white
    breadcrumbs*

Scrub the potatoes but do not peel them. Put them in a saucepan of cold water, add some salt and bring to the boil. Simmer for about 25 minutes or until just tender but still firm.

Drain the potatoes and rinse them under cold running water, then drain again and leave to cool completely. Chill.

Gently press a 4.5-cm / 2-inch round pastry cutter [US cookie cutter] into one side of each potato, not cutting all the way through (to within about 5 mm / ¹/₄ inch of the other side). Lift out the cutter, taking

the plug of potato with it. Carefully peel the potatoes.

Heat a pan of oil for deep frying to 200°C / 400°F.

Lightly beat the egg with a pinch of salt. Season the potatoes with salt and pepper, then dust all over with flour and shake off the excess. Dip into the egg wash, coating well, then coat with breadcrumbs.

Deep fry the potatoes for about 1 minute or until golden brown, turning them so they colour evenly. Drain on paper towels and serve hot.

TIPS

The potatoes can be cooked and shaped in advance and then coated and deep-fried just before serving. Or, you can fry them and keep them warm, uncovered, in a moderate oven.

When cutting the hollow in the potatoes, take care not to break the skin around the cut or the potatoes will fall apart.

MINTED NEW POTATOES

Serves 4

*700 g / 1¹/₂ lb new potatoes
6 sprigs of fresh mint*

*sea salt and freshly ground black pepper
45 g / 1¹/₂ oz / 3 tbsp unsalted butter*

Wash the potatoes well. Pull the mint leaves from the stalks; set the leaves aside.

Put the potatoes in a saucepan, cover with cold water and add the mint stalks and a pinch of salt. Bring to the boil, then cover and simmer for about 15 minutes or until the potatoes are tender.

Drain the potatoes and discard the mint stalks. Return them to the pan and toss over the heat to dry them, if necessary. Chop the mint leaves and add to the pan with the butter. Toss to coat the potatoes. Season with freshly ground sea salt and pepper and serve.

TIP

Choose new potatoes that are young and fresh: the skin should come off easily when you rub it with your thumb. The older the potatoes are, the harder their skin.

ROASTED VEGETABLES WITH ROSEMARY OR THYME

TIP

The addition of a little butter towards the end of the roasting time gives a wonderful flavour to the vegetables.

The best way to roast vegetables is in the pan with meat or a bird because the flavour and juices of the meat perfume the vegetables, and the taste of the vegetables penetrate the meat. This doesn't mean that you cannot roast vegetables without meat, of course.

You can roast almost any vegetable, either singly or several together. In a mixture, the majority should be root vegetables, and you should try to mix the colours.

The vegetables suggested here are the ones most suitable for roasting. Roasting times given are a guideline, but be sure to check for tenderness – there is nothing worse than very over-cooked vegetables. When roasting a mixture of vegetables, add them to the pan in sequence according to the suggested cooking time.

VEGETABLE	PREPARATION	COOKING TIME
Asparagus	peel the stalks	20 minutes
Broccoli	separate into large florets	30 minutes
Carrots	peel and leave whole, depending on size	45 minutes
Cauliflower	separate into large florets	40 minutes
Celeriac [US celery root]	peel and cut into cubes	45 minutes
Corn on the cob	leave whole, in husks	50 minutes
Courgette [US zucchini]	leave whole	25 minutes
Garlic heads	leave whole, unpeeled	50 minutes
Leeks	trim, wash and blanch†	30 minutes
Onions	peel and cut in half or quarters if large	45 minutes
Parsnips	peel and quarter	45 minutes
Potatoes	peel and blanch‡	50 minutes
Red sweet peppers	cut in half and seed	45 minutes
Sweet potatoes	peel and cut in half if large	40 minutes

Heat the oven to 200°C / 400°F / gas 6.

Heat a roasting pan over moderate heat, then pour enough groundnut oil [US peanut oil] or vegetable oil into the pan to make a film on the bottom. Add the vegetables and turn to coat with the oil. Season. Transfer to the oven and roast for the time suggested above, testing to see if they are done 5–10 minutes before the time is up – they should be just tender.

Add a few fresh rosemary or thyme sprigs halfway through the roasting time. Dot with a little unsalted butter 5–10 minutes before the end of the cooking.

When they are ready, remove the pan from the oven and drain the vegetables on paper towels. Discard the herbs. Separate the garlic cloves. Taste and adjust the seasoning before serving.

† Drop leeks into boiling salted water and blanch for a few seconds.
‡ Put potatoes into cold salted water, bring to the boil and blanch for 1 minute.

143

MEDITERRANEAN VEGETABLE RAGOÛT

Serves 4

Serve this with fish, poultry and beef. It is also very good as an accompaniment for vegetarian dishes.

2 red sweet peppers
100 ml / 3¹/₂ fl oz / 7 tbsp olive oil
1 onion
2 garlic cloves
100 g / 3¹/₂ oz mushrooms
2 courgettes [US zucchini]

1 small sprig of fresh rosemary
¹/₂ tsp sugar
¹/₂ tsp white wine vinegar
salt and freshly ground black pepper
4 ripe but firm plum tomatoes

Heat the oven to 220°C / 425°F / gas 7.

Rub the red peppers with a little olive oil and put them in a small casserole or roasting pan. Cover with a lid or foil and bake for 20 minutes.

Remove the casserole from the oven and set aside, covered, for 10 minutes. Turn the oven down to 180°C / 350°F / gas 4.

When the peppers are cool enough to handle, peel them. Discard the stalks, white ribs and seeds and cut the flesh into 1-cm / ¹/₂-inch squares.

Peel and finely chop the onion. Peel the garlic and chop to a paste (see page 13). Heat the remaining olive oil in a flame-proof casserole and cook the onion over low heat until soft and translucent, stirring often. Add the garlic and cook for 1 minute longer.

Cut the mushrooms into quarters. Cut the courgettes into 1-cm / ¹/₂-inch cubes. Add the mushrooms and courgettes to the casserole and cook for 2 minutes, stirring occasionally.

Add the red peppers to the casserole and stir well. Add the rosemary, sugar and vinegar, and season with salt and pepper.

Cover the casserole and transfer to the oven. Cook for 25 minutes, stirring frequently.

Meanwhile, peel the tomatoes and remove the seeds (see page 74). Cut the tomato flesh into 1-cm / ¹/₂-inch squares.

Stir the tomatoes into the ragoût. Taste and adjust the seasoning and discard the rosemary sprig before serving.

GRILLED VEGETABLES

Serves 4

These can also be cooked outdoors on a barbecue.

2 small heads of garlic
1 red sweet pepper
1 green sweet pepper
1 small kohlrabi, weighing about 200 g / 7 oz
1 medium-sized aubergine [US eggplant],
* weighing about 225 g / 8 oz*

2 medium-sized courgettes [US zucchini]
salt and freshly ground black pepper
100 ml / 3½ fl oz / 7 tbsp olive oil
2–3 sprigs of fresh rosemary
2–3 sprigs of fresh thyme

Cut each head of garlic across in half. Set the halves, cut side up, in a pan of cold water, bring to the boil and boil for 1 minute. Drain, then repeat this blanching two more times. Drain well.

Remove the stalks and seeds from the red and green peppers, then cut the flesh into triangles about 6 cm / 2½ inches long.

Peel the kohlrabi and cut into 8 rounds, each about 3-mm / ⅛-inch thick. Trim the stalk from the aubergine and cut lengthwise into 8 slices, each about 5-mm / ¼-inch thick. Trim the courgettes and cut each one into 4 slices, each about 3-mm / ⅛-inch thick. Spread out the slices on a large tray and sprinkle generously with salt and pepper. Set aside for 5 minutes, to draw out the liquid, then pat the vegetables dry with paper towels.

Heat the grill [US broiler] and grill pan with rack in place, or heat a ridged cast iron grill pan on top of the stove until it is very hot.

Pour the olive oil into a roasting pan or baking tray. Turn all the vegetables in the oil to coat, then transfer to the hot grill rack or pan. Grill them quickly on both sides until they are cooked and golden brown: the kohlrabi and garlic will take about 10 minutes, the aubergine and peppers 7–10 minutes, and the courgettes 4–5 minutes.

Return the garlic and vegetables to the pan of oil and add the herbs. Set aside until needed.

Just before serving, warm the grilled garlic and vegetables in the oven or under the grill.

MIXED SPRING VEGETABLES

Baby vegetables are tender so they need only be cooked briefly. Select 3 or 4 vegetables from those suggested here, so you have a good combination of colours. You'll need 450–600 g / 1–1¼ lb in total to serve 4. Cook each vegetable separately, ahead of time if that is convenient, then finish for serving.

BABY ASPARAGUS: Prepare the asparagus (see page 90). Cook in simmering salted water for 2½ minutes or until just tender but still firm. Drain and refresh in iced water, then drain again well.

BABY BEETROOT [US BEETS]: Cook in simmering salted water for 10–12 minutes or until just tender but still firm. Drain well and refresh under cold running water, then peel.

BABY CARROTS: Scrub or peel, leaving a little of the green end. Melt a little butter in a small saucepan and add a pinch of sugar and the carrots. Cook over a moderate heat for 3 minutes, stirring often. Add 5–6 tbsp of water and season with salt and pepper. Cover the pan and cook over a very low heat for about 6 minutes or until the carrots are just tender but still have some bite.

BABY CAULIFLOWER: Trim off most of the leaves and the base of the core. Cook in simmering salted water for about 4 minutes or until just tender but still firm. Drain and refresh in iced water, then drain again well.

BABY COURGETTES [US ZUCCHINI]: Trim the ends. Cook in simmering salted water for about 3 minutes or until just tender but still firm. Drain and refresh in iced water, then drain again well.

SMALL BUTTON MUSHROOMS: Trim the stalks. Melt a little butter in a small saucepan, add the mushrooms and season with salt and pepper. Cover and cook over a moderately low heat for 2 minutes.

BUTTON OR BABY ONIONS [US PEARL ONIONS]: Peel. Cook in simmering salted water for 4–5 minutes or until tender but still firm. Drain and refresh in iced water, then drain again well.

FRESH PEAS: If very small, leave in the pod; otherwise, shell them. Cook in simmering salted water for 2–3 minutes or until just tender but still firm. Drain and refresh in iced water, then drain again well.

BABY TURNIPS: Use only small ones as large turnips have an inferior flavour. Scrub or peel, leaving a little of the green end. Melt a little butter in a small saucepan and add a pinch of sugar and the turnips. Cook over a moderate heat for 3 minutes, stirring often. Add 5–6 tbsp water and season with salt and pepper. Cover the pan and cook over low heat for about 10 minutes or until the turnips are just tender but still have some bite.

To finish: Warm carrots and turnips in their cooking liquid. Heat beetroot separately in butter. Toss all the other vegetables in hot butter. Season with salt and pepper and serve.

TIP

An attractive presentation is to pile a mixture of baby vegetables in deep-fried potatoes (see recipe on page 142).

VEGETABLE SPRING ROLLS

Makes 8

2 eggs
salt and freshly ground black pepper
2 tbsp vegetable oil, plus more for deep frying
6 spring onions [US scallions]
90 g / 3 oz mange-tout [US snow peas]
60 g / 2 oz fresh oyster mushrooms
2 carrots
90 g / 3 oz Chinese leaves [US Napa cabbage] or Chinese cabbage

2 garlic cloves
2 tbsp sesame oil
1 tbsp finely chopped fresh root ginger
75 g / 2¹/₂ oz / ³/₄ cup fresh beansprouts
1 tbsp hoisin sauce
2 tbsp soy sauce
1 tbsp Chicken Essence (see page 14)
8 squares of filo pastry dough, each about 20 x 20 cm / 8 x 8 inches

Put 1 of the eggs in a bowl. Separate the second egg and set the yolk aside. Add the white to the bowl and mix the contents together with a fork and season with salt and pepper.

Heat 2 tsp of the vegetable oil in a frying pan over moderate heat and fry half of the egg mixture to make a firm, thin omelette. Remove from the pan and leave to cool. Make a second omelette in the same way. When the omelettes are cold, cut them into quarters and stack them. Roll up loosely, then cut across the roll into thin matchsticks.

Trim the spring onions, mange-tout and mushrooms. Peel the carrots. Cut the spring onions, mange-tout, mushrooms, carrots and Chinese leaves into thin shreds. Peel the garlic and chop to a paste (see page 13).

Heat a wok or heavy-based frying pan over high heat and then add the remaining vegetable oil and the sesame oil. Add the spring onions, garlic and ginger and stir-fry for 2 minutes. Add the remaining prepared vegetables and the beansprouts and stir-fry for 2 more minutes.

Remove the wok from the heat and stir in the sauces and chicken essence. Season with salt and pepper. Gently mix in the omelette strips. Tip out of the wok on to a tray, spread out and leave to cool.

Lightly beat the reserved egg yolk with ¹/₂ tsp water.

Divide the vegetable mixture among the squares of filo pastry, spooning it in a wide strip down the centre. Brush all the edges of the pastry square with the egg wash. Fold one side of the pastry square over the filling, then fold up the top and bottom. Finally, fold the other side over the top, to make a flattened parcel that is about 6 cm / 2¹/₂ inches wide and 16 to 18 cm / 6 ¹/₂ to 7 inches long. Press to seal well.

Heat a pan of vegetable oil for deep frying to 200°C / 400°F.

Fry the spring rolls for about 1 minute or until they are golden brown, turning them so they colour evenly. Drain on paper towels and serve, cut diagonally in half from corner to corner.

TEMPURA VEGETABLES

Serves 4

1 courgette [US zucchini]
¹/₂ medium-sized aubergine [US eggplant]
  or 3 baby aubergines
1 red sweet pepper

vegetable oil for deep frying
4 cauliflower florets
300 ml / ¹/₂ pint / 1¹/₄ cups White Batter
  (see page 18)

Trim the courgette and aubergine and cut them diagonally into 3-mm / ¹/₈-inch slices. Remove the core and seeds from the red pepper and cut the flesh into 5-cm / 2-inch long triangles. Set aside.

Heat oil for deep frying to 160°C / 325°F.

Dip the courgette and aubergine slices, pepper triangles and cauliflower florets into the batter, then deep-fry, a few pieces at a time, for about 3 minutes or until golden brown on all sides. Drain on paper towels and serve hot.

BAVARIAN CABBAGE

Serves 4

This is a delightful vegetable and it goes well with pork and grilled fish.

350 g / 12 oz white cabbage
1 onion
4 slices of smoked streaky bacon [US Canadian bacon]
2 tbsp vegetable oil

150 ml / ¹/₄ pint / ²/₃ cup Chicken Essence
  (see page 14)
1 small sprig of fresh thyme
1 small sprig of fresh rosemary
¹/₂ tsp caraway seeds
salt and freshly ground black pepper

Remove any damaged outside leaves from the cabbage. Cut it into wedges and cut out the core. Slice each wedge across into fine strips.

Drop the strips of cabbage into a saucepan of boiling salted water and simmer for 30 seconds. Drain and refresh in iced water. Drain again well.

Heat the oven to 170°C / 325°F / gas 3.

Peel and finely chop the onion. Remove any rind from the bacon, then cut across into fine strips.

Heat the oil in a small flameproof casserole over low heat and cook the onion until soft and translucent, stirring often. Add the bacon and cook over moderate heat for 1 minute. Stir in the cabbage. Pour in the chicken essence and add the herbs and caraway seeds. Season with salt and pepper.

Cover the casserole and transfer it to the oven. Braise for 20 minutes or until the cabbage is tender but still firm to the bite.

Drain the cabbage mixture in a colander set in a saucepan. Set the cabbage aside. Boil the cooking liquid until reduced to a glaze. Remove and discard the herb stalks.

Stir the cabbage into the glaze, and taste and adjust the seasoning. Serve hot.

TIP
If you cook the cabbage until it is only just tender, then cool it and add a little sherry vinaigrette (see page 21), you can serve it as a salad.

PURÉE OF BRUSSELS SPROUTS

Serves 4

500 g / 1 lb 2 oz Brussels sprouts
2 shallots
1/2 garlic clove
15 g / 1/2 oz / 1 tbsp unsalted butter

1 tbsp vegetable oil
300 ml / 1/2 pint / 1 1/4 cups double cream
  [US heavy whipping cream]

Trim the sprouts, discarding discoloured leaves. Cook in boiling salted water for 10 minutes or until very tender. Drain well.

Meanwhile, peel and finely chop the shallots. Peel the garlic and chop to a paste (see page 13). Heat the butter and oil in a saucepan over low heat and cook the shallots until soft, stirring often. Add the garlic and cook gently for 1 minute longer.

Add the Brussels sprouts to the shallots.

Stir in the cream. Bring to the boil and boil for 5 minutes or until the cream has reduced by half. Remove and reserve one-third of the sprouts. Purée the remaining sprout mixture in a food processor and put it into a clean pan. Roughly chop the reserved sprouts and stir into the purée.

Reheat gently. Taste and adjust the seasoning before serving.

WHITE BEAN STEW

Serves 4

150 g / 5 oz / 3/4 cup dried white haricot beans
  [US dried navy or Great Northern beans]
1 onion
1 garlic clove
1/2 fresh hot red chilli pepper
4 slices of smoked streaky bacon [US Canadian
  bacon]
2 tbsp olive oil

1/2 tsp sugar
1 tbsp tomato paste
1/2 bay leaf
250 ml / 8 fl oz / 1 cup Chicken Essence
  (see page 14)
1 tsp white wine vinegar
salt and freshly ground black pepper

Soak the beans overnight in cold water. Drain and rinse well.

Peel and finely chop the onion. Peel the garlic and chop to a paste (see page 13). Finely chop the chilli. Remove rind from the bacon, then cut across into fine strips.

Heat the oil in a saucepan over low heat and cook the onion until soft and translucent, stirring often. Add the garlic, chilli and sugar and cook for 1 minute longer.

Stir in the tomato paste and cook for another minute.

Add the beans, bacon and bay leaf and pour in the chicken essence. Bring to the boil, then reduce the heat, cover and simmer for about 1 1/4 hours or until the beans are tender. If necessary, add a little more essence or water if the beans look too dry.

Stir in the vinegar and season with salt and pepper. Discard the bay leaf before serving.

SPINACH SPÄTZLE

Serves 4

180 g / 6 oz fresh spinach
200 g / 7 oz / 1 1/3 cups flour
3 eggs
2 tbsp vegetable oil

a small pinch of freshly grated nutmeg
salt and freshly ground black pepper
60 g / 2 oz / 4 tbsp unsalted butter

Pull the stalks off the spinach leaves, then wash the leaves well. Blanch them in boiling salted water for 30 seconds, then drain and refresh in iced water. Drain the spinach well. When it is cool enough to handle, squeeze it to remove all excess water. Purée the spinach in a blender or food processor, and squeeze again to be sure the purée is quite dry.

Sift the flour into a bowl and make a well in the centre. Add the spinach purée, eggs, half the oil, and the nutmeg. Season with salt and pepper. Mix well together, slowly drawing in the flour from the sides, to make a very elastic paste. Beat with a wooden spoon for 3 minutes or until air bubbles form in the paste.

Bring a large wide saucepan of salted water to the boil and add the remaining oil.

Dampen a thin wooden board that is about 25 x 20 cm / 10 x 8 inches. Spread a small amount of the spinach paste thinly on the board. Dip the whole board briefly in the boiling water, then lift it out and, using a palette knife [US metal spatula], quickly scrape off long thin strips of the paste directly into the boiling water. Cook for about 1 minute.

With a slotted spoon, lift out the spätzle and refresh in iced water. Drain again and set aside. Continue cooking the spätzle in this way. When all the spätzle have been cooked, pat them dry with paper towels.

Melt the butter in a frying pan over moderate heat. Toss the spätzle in the melted butter until hot and lightly golden. Season with salt and pepper, and serve.

TIPS

When scraping the paste from the wooden board, clean your spatula from time to time and dip it into the boiling water.

Stir the spätzle often in the boiling water so they cook evenly and don't stick together.

Instead of using fresh leaf spinach, you can substitute frozen spinach purée.

You can make the spätzle without spinach, in which case you will need a little more egg.

THAI RICE

Serves 4

1 small onion
15 g / 1/2 oz / 1 tbsp unsalted butter
200 g / 7 oz / 1 heaped cup Thai fragrant
  rice

350 ml / 12 fl oz / 1 1/2 cups Chicken Essence
  (see page 14)
a pinch of saffron threads
salt and freshly ground pepper

Heat the oven to 180°C / 350°F / gas 4. Peel and finely chop the onion. Heat the butter in a small flameproof casserole over low heat and cook the onion until translucent, stirring often. Stir in the rice, then

add the chicken essence, saffron threads, and salt and pepper to taste. Bring to the boil, cover tightly and transfer to the oven. Bake for 10-15 minutes or until the rice is tender and the essence has been absorbed.

TIP

Check frequently towards the end of cooking as the rice overcooks easily.

SOPHIE'S COUSCOUS

Serves 4

This recipe originated in Cyprus (as did my assistant, Sophie), where it is used as a stuffing for the Christmas turkey. It is not at all like the couscous of North Africa. The unique slightly sweet and nutty flavour of couscous goes very well with dishes based on poultry or game birds as well as with lamb or fish.

1 onion
50 g / 1³/4 oz livers from chicken, turkey or game bird
100 g / 3¹/2 oz / 1 cup slivered almonds
3 tbsp groundnut oil [US peanut oil]
2 'nests' of vermicelli
150 ml / ¹/4 pint / ²/3 cup dry white wine

250 ml / 8 fl oz / 1 cup Chicken Essence (see page 14)
2.5-cm / 1-inch piece of cinnamon stick
salt and freshly ground black pepper
250 g / 8¹/2 oz / 1¹/2 cups couscous
chopped fresh flat-leaf (Italian) parsley, to finish (optional)

Peel and finely chop the onion. Clean the livers and cut them into bite-size pieces if they are large. Coarsely chop the almonds.

Heat the oil in a saucepan over a low heat and cook the onion until soft and translucent, stirring often. Crush the vermicelli finely and add to the pan. Stir over medium heat until golden brown. Add the livers, almonds and wine and bring to the boil. Simmer for 1 minute.

Add the chicken essence, cinnamon and some salt and pepper and bring to the boil.

Add the couscous and stir for 1 minute. When the mixture returns to the boil, reduce the heat to very low, cover the pan and simmer for 10–15 minutes or until all the couscous is tender and all the liquid has been absorbed.

Remove the pan from the heat and set aside, covered, for 5 minutes. Discard the cinnamon, fluff the couscous grains, and taste and adjust the seasoning. If you like, fold some chopped parsley through the couscous before serving.

MUSHROOM-FILLED PASTRY LEAVES

Makes 4

This is a very attractive and delicious garnish.

100 g / 3¹/2 oz Puff Pastry (see page 27)
1 egg yolk

For the wild mushroom filling
1 shallot
¹/2 small garlic clove
a little unsalted butter and vegetable oil

45 g / 1¹/2 oz fresh wild mushrooms or tiny
*   button mushrooms*
salt and freshly ground black pepper
1 tbsp Madeira wine
3¹/2 tbsp double cream [US heavy whipping
*   cream]*
1 tsp chopped fresh parsley

Heat the oven to 220°C / 425°F / gas 7.

Roll out the puff pastry to about 5-mm / ¹/4-inch thickness and cut out 4 leaf shapes, 4 cm / 1¹/2 inches wide and 7 cm / 2³/4 inches long. With the tip of a sharp knife, score a smaller leaf shape on the top of each pastry, about 5 mm / ¹/4 inch in from the edge. Then arrange the pastries on a baking sheet.

Lightly beat the egg yolk with ¹/2 tsp water. Brush this egg glaze over the tops of the pastries. Bake them for about 15 minutes or until well risen and golden brown.

Leave them to cool slightly, then slice off the central leaf-shaped 'lid' and remove the undercooked pastry from the centre to make a hollow. Keep the pastry shells and lids warm.

For the wild mushroom filling, peel and finely chop the shallot. Peel the garlic and

chop to a paste (see page 13). Heat a little butter and oil in a frying pan over low heat and cook the shallot until soft and translucent, stirring often. Add the garlic and cook gently for 1 minute longer.

Trim and clean the mushrooms, then slice them. Add to the pan and season with salt and pepper. Cook over moderate heat, stirring constantly, for about 3 minutes. Add the Madeira and boil until reduced to a glaze. Stir in the cream. Bring back to the boil, then simmer until the liquid has reduced by half.

Remove the mushrooms with a slotted spoon. Boil the liquid in the pan until thick, then stir in the mushrooms and parsley. Taste and adjust the seasoning.

Fill the pastry shells with the mushroom mixture, replace the lids and serve.

TIP
The mushroom-filled pastry leaves would make a delightful first course during the mushroom season. Use 150 g / 5 oz puff pastry, and increase the size of the pastry cases by about half. Then use 90 g / 3 oz mushrooms, 2 tbsp Madeira and 100 ml / 3¹/2 fl oz / 7 tbsp cream to make the filling.

LAST COURSES

IT is surprising that in this day and age, when we would all like to be somewhat thinner and trimmer, that the popularity of desserts and all sweet things is on the increase. This is very reassuring to me because who in their right mind would throw away something that gives so much happiness? And something which can be so intriguingly delicious in its flavours and aromas? A dessert of some kind is surely the fitting end to a meal.

What is of concern is that the great art of making desserts has almost gone in the home kitchen. Yet a dinner without a dessert, or tea without pastries and cakes, is unthinkable. The preparation of cakes, brûlées, pastries, sorbets and ice creams does, of course, take patience and time, and you might not get it right the first time. But believe me, the rewards are a delight in the long run.

Once you have eaten a slice of warm cherry tart, or a dish of summer fruit marinated in wine, or a scoop of steamed sultana pudding, it must become clear that there is only one way forward, and that is to eat more of it!

CRÈME BRÛLÉE WITH BERRIES AND SAUTERNES

Serves 6

Unlike many versions of this popular dessert, my crème brûlée is served warm. The caramel topping, which is usually a hard crust on top, is only just set.

7 egg yolks
150 ml / ¼ pint / ⅔ cup sweet white wine, preferably Sauternes
1 tbsp icing sugar [US confectioners' sugar]
250 ml / 8 fl oz / 1 cup double cream [US heavy whipping cream]

90 g / 3 oz / ¾ cup fresh raspberries or other berries in season
30 g / 1 oz / 2 tbsp caster sugar [US granulated sugar]
Almond Biscotti (see box), to serve

Heat the oven to 150°C / 300°F / gas 2.

Combine the egg yolks and wine in a bowl and lightly whisk them together. Sift the icing sugar over the surface and stir until it has dissolved. Gently stir in the cream. There should be no froth on the surface of the mixture.

Ladle the mixture into six 8.5-cm / 3¼-inch diameter ramekins. Divide the raspberries among the dishes.

Set the dishes in a roasting pan and add enough hot water to the pan to come halfway up the sides of the dishes. Transfer the pan to the oven and bake for about 30 minutes or until the creams are just set. The water should not boil so reduce the oven temperature slightly if necessary.

Remove the dishes from the pan of water and leave to cool slightly.

Heat the grill [US broiler].

Sprinkle the surface of each cream evenly with caster sugar. Set the dishes on a baking sheet and grill for 1–2 minutes or until the sugar has melted and caramelized. Set aside to cool to body temperature.

Serve with the almond biscotti.

ALMOND BISCOTTI

Toast 90 g / 3 oz / ⅔ cup whole blanched almonds (see page 84). Finely grind 1 star anise in a spice mill or with a mortar and pestle. Sift 200 g / 7 oz / 1⅓ cups flour, 120 g / 4 oz / 1 cup icing sugar [US confectioners' sugar] and a pinch of salt into a bowl. Make a well in the centre. Lightly beat 2 whole eggs with 1 egg yolk and add to the well in the dry ingredients. Add the ground star anise and the grated zest of ½ unwaxed lemon and ½ unwaxed orange. Mix together to make a sticky dough. Knead in the toasted almonds. Shape into a 4-cm / 1½-inch diameter log and wrap in baking parchment. Refrigerate for 1 hour.

Heat the oven to 180°C / 350°F / gas 4. Set the log, still in its parchment, on a baking sheet and bake for 50–55 minutes or until golden brown. Allow to cool, then cut into very thin slices, about 2 mm. Lay them on a wire rack to dry.

PLUM AND FRANGIPANE TART WITH STREUSEL

Serves 6

This is my mother's recipe. It can be served as a dessert, with whipped or clotted cream, or – even better – plain, with a cup of tea in the afternoon.

125 ml / 4 fl oz / ½ cup milk
15 g / ½ oz fresh yeast
3 tbsp vegetable oil
250 g / 9 oz / 2¼ cups strong plain flour [US all-purpose flour]
2 tsp caster sugar [US granulated sugar]
1 tsp salt
900 g / 2 lb ripe but firm plums

For the frangipane
90 g / 3 oz / 6 tbsp unsalted butter, at room temperature
90 g / 3 oz / 7 tbsp caster sugar [US granulated sugar]

2 eggs
90 g / 3 oz / 1 cup ground almonds
25 g / ¾ oz / 3 tbsp plain flour [US all-purpose flour]

For the streusel
120 g / 4 oz / ¾ cup plain flour [US all-purpose flour]
3 tbsp caster sugar [US granulated sugar]
1 tsp ground allspice
90 g / 3 oz / 6 tbsp cold unsalted butter

Warm the milk to lukewarm and pour it into a large bowl. Add the yeast and mash with a spoon until creamy. Stir in the oil. Leave in a warm place for 10 minutes.

Sift the flour, sugar and salt into the bowl and mix to make a smooth dough. Turn out on to a lightly floured surface and knead for 8–10 minutes or until smooth and elastic. Put the dough into an oiled bowl, cover with oiled cling film [US plastic wrap] and leave to rise in a warm place for 40 minutes or until doubled in bulk.

Meanwhile, make the frangipane. With an electric mixer at high speed, cream the butter with the sugar until pale and fluffy. Beat the eggs with a fork, then gradually beat them into the creamed mixture at medium speed. Sift the almonds and flour over the surface and fold in until mixed.

Cut the plums in half and remove the stones [US pits].

Butter a 23- x 33-cm / 9- x 13-inch Swiss roll tin [US jelly roll pan]. Knead the dough lightly, then on a floured surface roll it out to a rectangle. Put it in the centre of the buttered tin and press it out to line the bottom and sides of the tin. Spread the frangipane over the bottom of the dough case. Chill for 20 minutes.

Heat the oven to 180°C / 350°F / gas 4.

For the streusel, combine the flour, sugar and allspice in a bowl. Cut the butter into small cubes and rub into the dry ingredients until the mixture resembles large pea-size crumbs.

Arrange the plum halves in rows on top of the frangipane. Sprinkle the streusel evenly over the top. Bake for about 55 minutes or until the pastry and streusel topping are golden brown. Serve warm, cut into large squares.

OVER PAGE
Plum and Frangipane Tart with Streusel

GOOSEBERRY DUMPLINGS

Serves 4

3 1/2 tbsp milk
175 g / 6 oz / 1 1/2 cups strong plain flour
   [US all-purpose flour]
7 g / 1/4 oz fresh yeast (a 2-cm / 3/4-inch cube)
2 1/2 tbsp caster sugar [US granulated sugar]
a pinch of salt
30 g / 1 oz / 2 tbsp unsalted butter, at room
   temperature
1 whole egg

1 egg yolk
2 tbsp vegetable oil
1 tsp ground cinnamon

For the gooseberry filling
160 g / 5 1/2 oz gooseberries
4 tbsp sugar
1 tbsp cornflour [US cornstarch]

TIP

These dumplings can be filled with other fruits such as cherries, plums or apricots.

Warm the milk to lukewarm. Combine 60 g / 2 oz / 1/2 cup of the flour, the yeast and milk in a bowl and mix to make a dough. Leave in a warm place for 10 minutes.

Add the remaining flour, 1 tbsp of the sugar, the salt, butter, egg and egg yolk to the yeast dough and mix until smooth. Knead the dough for about 5 minutes or until it is smooth and elastic. Put it into a plastic bag and leave to rise in a warm place for about 1 hour or until doubled in bulk.

Meanwhile, make the gooseberry filling. Wash the gooseberries, then trim off the tops and tails. Put them in a heavy-based saucepan with the sugar and a little water (just 5 mm / 1/4 inch deep) and cook over low heat until the gooseberries are soft, stirring occasionally. Mix the cornflour with 1 1/2 tbsp water until smooth, then add to the gooseberries and cook, stirring, until the juices have thickened. Remove from the heat and set aside.

Heat the oven to 200°C / 400°F / gas 6.

Pour 1/2 tbsp of oil into each of 4 individual baking dishes that are about 6.5 cm / 2 1/2 inches wide and 3.5 cm / 1 1/2 inches deep (oeuf en cocotte dishes or muffin tins are ideal). Put the dishes into the oven to heat.

Knead the dough lightly, then divide it into 4 equal pieces. On a lightly floured surface, roll out each piece to a disc 5 mm / 1/4 inch thick. Spoon the gooseberries and a little juice into the centre of the discs. Gather up the edges over the filling, like a sack, and twist and press together to seal.

When the oil is sizzling hot, put a dumpling in each dish. Bake for about 15 minutes or until the dumplings are slightly puffed and deep golden brown.

Mix together the cinnamon and remaining sugar on a plate.

Remove the dumplings from the dishes and turn the bases and sides in the cinnamon sugar to coat. Serve immediately, with the remaining gooseberry juices and cream or a fruit sauce.

SALZBURGER SOUFFLÉ DUMPLINGS

Serves 4

This dessert is so popular in Austria that songs have been written about it!

200 ml / 7 fl oz / 7/8 cup double cream
  [US heavy whipping cream]
100 g / 3 1/2 oz / 7 tbsp unsalted butter
1 vanilla pod [US vanilla bean]
5 tsp vanilla sugar
2 tbsp eau-de-vie de framboise (raspberry
  liqueur)

2 whole eggs
5 tbsp caster sugar [US granulated sugar]
20 g / 2/3 oz / 2 1/2 tbsp flour
2 egg whites
icing sugar [US confectioners' sugar],
  to finish

Put the cream and butter in a heavy-based saucepan. Split the vanilla pod open and scrape the seeds from inside into the cream. Add the pod to the cream. Bring to the boil, stirring to melt the butter. Stir in the vanilla sugar until it has dissolved, then remove from the heat. Stir in the eau-de-vie de framboise. Remove and discard the vanilla pod.

Pour the cream sauce into a 23-cm / 9-inch round earthenware baking dish to make a 1-cm / 1/2-inch deep layer. Set aside.

Heat the oven to 220°C / 425°F / gas 7.

Separate the whole eggs. Combine the egg yolks, 1 tbsp of the caster sugar and 1 tbsp water in a bowl and whisk until pale and thick and doubled in volume. Sift the flour and fold gently into the mixture.

In a large clean bowl, whisk the 4 egg whites with the remaining caster sugar to a soft peak. Stir a spoonful of the whites into the egg yolk mixture, then gently fold in the remaining whites with a large metal spoon.

With a large spoon, scoop the soufflé mixture and place in 4 or 8 neat heaps, just touching, on the sauce in the baking dish.

Bake for 12 minutes or until puffed and light golden brown.

Sprinkle with sifted icing sugar and serve immediately.

ORANGE QUARK SOUFFLÉ

Serves 6

4 oranges
2 eggs, size 2 [US extra large]
300 g / 10 oz / 1 1/4 cups quark
finely grated zest of 1 unwaxed lemon
5 tsp cornflour [US cornstarch]
2 tbsp light rum
6 tbsp icing sugar [US confectioners' sugar]

1 egg white, from a size-2 egg [US extra large egg]
300 ml / 1/2 pint / 1 1/4 cups freshly squeezed orange juice
strips of Caramelized Orange Zest (see box), to decorate

Peel the oranges and cut out the segments (see page 72).

Prepare 6 individual soufflé dishes that are about 8 cm / 3 1/4 inches in diameter and 3.5 cm / 1 1/2 inches deep (see tip).

Heat the oven to 220°C / 425°F / gas 7.

Separate the 2 whole eggs. Mix together the 2 egg yolks, the quark, lemon zest, 2 1/2 tsp of the cornflour, the rum and half of the icing sugar in a bowl.

In another large clean bowl, whisk the 3 egg whites with the remaining icing sugar to a stiff peak. Stir a spoonful of the whites into the quark mixture to loosen it, then gently fold in the remaining whites with a large metal spoon.

Divide the soufflé mixture among the prepared dishes. Set the dishes in a roasting pan and pour enough cold water into the pan to come halfway up the sides of the dishes. Place in the oven and bake for 15 minutes or until well risen and golden.

Mix the remaining cornflour with 2 tbsp of the orange juice. Strain the remaining juice into a saucepan and heat, then stir in the cornflour mixture. Simmer, stirring, until thickened. Just before serving, add the orange segments and heat through.

Remove the segments and arrange around the edge of the warmed plates. If using the caramelized orange zest, put a strip on each orange segment.

Remove the soufflés from the oven and lift them out of the pan of water. Holding each dish in a towel, loosen the sides of the soufflé with a small sharp knife and turn it out upside down in the centre of a plate. Spoon the orange sauce around the soufflés and serve immediately.

CARAMELIZED ORANGE ZEST

Pare the zest very thinly from 2 unwaxed oranges, being careful not to take any of the white pith. Cut the zest into very thin strips. Blanch the strips of zest in a pan of boiling water for 30 seconds, then drain. Combine 150 g / 5 oz / 3/4 cup sugar and 100 ml / 3 1/2 fl oz / 7 tbsp water in a saucepan. (Or you can use half water and half grenadine.) Bring to the boil, stirring to dissolve the sugar. Add the strips of zest and simmer for about 10 minutes or until the sugar syrup has reduced by about half. Remove from the heat and allow to cool. Leave the zest in the sugar syrup until ready to use.

TIPS

When preparing the soufflé dishes, be sure to butter the inside and the top edge well and to sugar it so the soufflé will not stick when it is rising during baking. Chill before using.

You can prepare the quark mixture up to 12 hours in advance and keep it, tightly covered, in the refrigerator. Fold in the whisked egg whites just before baking. Time the baking of the soufflés carefully so they can be served right away – they will not wait without falling.

Quark is a smooth, soft cheese that ranges in fat content from medium to completely fat-free. It is similar to cottage cheese in flavour. If no quark is available, you can substitute 260 g / 9 oz / 1 cup cottage cheese.

RIGHT
Orange Quark Soufflé

TAPIOCA PUDDING

Serves 4

Tapioca pudding is the most forgotten pudding there is! I am sure that if you try this delicious and easily-prepared recipe, it will become a firm favourite on your short list of most-used desserts.

75 g / 2¹/₂ oz / ¹/₂ cup tapioca
600 ml / 1 pint / 2¹/₂ cups milk
1 vanilla pod [US vanilla bean]
4 whole cloves
4 tbsp sugar
2 egg yolks

125 ml / 4 fl oz / ¹/₂ cup double cream
   [US heavy whipping cream]

For the poached peaches
200 g / 7 oz / 1 cup sugar
2 large, ripe but firm peaches

Put the tapioca and milk in a heavy-based saucepan and set aside for 20 minutes.

Meanwhile, poach the peaches. Combine the sugar and 250 ml / 8 fl oz / 1 cup water in a saucepan. Heat, stirring to dissolve the sugar, then bring to the boil and boil for 1 minute. Cut a cross in the skin at the base of each peach. Add the peaches to the syrup and poach over moderate heat for 10 seconds. Lift them out with a slotted spoon and immerse in iced water. When they are cool enough to handle, slip off their skins.

Return the peeled peaches to the syrup and poach until they are just tender – 5 minutes or so, according to ripeness. Drain. When the peaches are cool enough to handle, cut them in half and remove the stones [US pits]. Put a peach half in each small flameproof serving dish. Set aside.

Add the split-open vanilla pod and cloves to the tapioca mixture and bring to the boil. Reduce the heat and simmer gently for about 10 minutes or until the tapioca is tender and swollen in size. Stir frequently to prevent it sticking.

Heat the grill [US broiler].

Remove and discard the vanilla pod and cloves from the tapioca mixture. Mix together the sugar, egg yolks and cream. Add to the tapioca mixture and bring back just to boiling point, stirring constantly.

Pour the tapioca pudding over the peach halves. Glaze the surface quickly under the grill, and serve.

CRÊPES WITH RICE PUDDING AND FRESH FRUIT

Serves 4

This is one of my all-time favourite desserts. It can be served with any kind of fresh fruit in season, or in winter with a warm fruit compote.

200 g / 7 oz mixed summer fruit such as raspberries, blackcurrants, redcurrants, blueberries and blackberries
Raspberry Sauce (see page 170), to serve
icing sugar [US confectioners' sugar], to finish

For the rice pudding
900 ml / 1 1/2 pints / 3 3/4 cups milk
1-cm / 1/2-inch piece of cinnamon stick
75 g / 2 1/2 oz / 6 tbsp short-grain 'pudding' rice
2–3 tbsp quark or ricotta cheese

3 tbsp caster sugar [US granulated sugar] or more to taste

For the crêpes
20 g / 2/3 oz / 4 tsp unsalted butter
60 g / 2 oz / 7 tbsp flour
25 g / 3/4 oz / 2 tbsp caster sugar [US granulated sugar]
a pinch of salt
1 egg
125 ml / 4 fl oz / 1/2 cup milk
3–4 tbsp vegetable oil

Rinse the berries and dry them carefully. Set aside.

To make the rice pudding, put the milk and cinnamon stick in a heavy-based saucepan and bring to the boil. Rinse the rice well under cold running water and drain, then add to the milk. Simmer for about 35 minutes or until the rice is tender and the milk absorbed, stirring frequently.

Meanwhile, make the crêpes. Melt the butter in a small pan and cook, swirling it around in the pan, until it is very lightly browned. Remove from the heat and allow to cool. Whisk together the flour, sugar, salt and egg. Gradually whisk in the milk and then the melted butter. If the batter is at all lumpy, pass it through a fine sieve.

Heat some of the oil in a 14-cm / 15 1/2-inch crêpe pan. Ladle enough batter into

the pan to make a thin coating, tilting and rotating the pan to spread the batter evenly. Cook until the crêpe is lightly browned, then turn or flip it over and cook the other side briefly. Turn the crêpe on to a plate and cover with a towel to keep it warm. Make 7 more crêpes in the same way, stacking them on the plate. Keep warm.

When the rice is cooked, discard the cinnamon stick. Stir in the quark. Sweeten with sugar to taste and allow to cool slightly.

Place 2 crêpes on each warmed plate, fill them with the rice pudding and fold over in half. Pour a little raspberry sauce around the crêpes. Garnish with the berries and dust lightly with icing sugar. Serve immediately.

HOT CHOCOLATE PUDDING

Serves 4

Chocolate and mint are a classic and extremely successful combination.

*150 g / 5 oz good-quality plain chocolate
[US bittersweet chocolate]
15 g / 1/2 oz / 1 tbsp unsalted butter
3 eggs
3 tbsp caster sugar [US superfine sugar]*

*soft unsalted butter for the dishes
icing sugar [US confectioners' sugar],
to finish
Mint Custard Sauce (see page 25), to serve*

Melt the chocolate with the butter in a heavy-based saucepan over very low heat. Remove the mixture from the heat and pour into a bowl.

Separate the eggs, taking care not to have any trace of yolk in the whites. Beat the egg yolks into the melted chocolate.

In a large clean bowl, whisk the egg whites with the caster sugar to a stiff peak. Stir a spoonful of the whites into the chocolate mixture to loosen it, then fold in the remaining whites with a metal spoon. Cover and refrigerate for 1½–2 hours.

Heat the oven to 220°C / 425°F / gas 7.

Generously butter the insides of four 8.5-cm / 3¼-inch diameter ramekins.

Spoon the chocolate mixture into the ramekins (it should come to 5 mm / ¼ inch from the top). Bake for 15 minutes or until risen. Remove from the oven and set aside in a warm place to rest for 15 minutes.

Loosen the sides of each pudding with a small sharp knife, then turn it out into your hand. Set the pudding right side up in the centre of a warmed plate. Dust lightly with icing sugar and serve, with the mint custard sauce.

TIPS

It is important to leave the puddings to rest before turning them out. They will shrink slightly on cooling, and will thus be easier to unmould.

If you prefer, you can serve the puddings in the dishes. They will taste just as delicious.

RIGHT
Hot Chocolate Pudding

BRIOCHE AND BUTTER PUDDING

Serves 4

Brioche makes a lighter version of traditional bread and butter pudding. The butter caramel on the bottom of the dish will spread throughout the pudding during baking, adding extra depth of flavour.

100 g / 3¹/₂ oz / nearly 1 cup dried apricots
3 tbsp brandy
100 g / 3¹/₂ oz / ¹/₂ cup caster sugar [US granulated sugar]
¹/₂ tsp liquid glucose [US light corn syrup]
120 g / 4 oz / 1 stick (8 tbsp) unsalted butter, at room temperature

100 g / 3¹/₂ oz brioche loaf
3 eggs
250 ml / 8 fl oz / 1 cup milk
2 tbsp apricot jam

Put the apricots in a bowl and sprinkle with the brandy and 6 tbsp water. Set aside to soak overnight or until softened and plump.

Drain the apricots if necessary, reserving the liquid, and cut them into small dice.

Warm a small heavy-based saucepan over very low heat. Put half of the sugar in the pan and melt it gently. Increase the heat to moderate and cook, stirring occasionally, until the sugar caramelizes to a rich golden brown. Stir in the glucose and half the butter, a little at a time.

Pour the butter caramel into a soufflé dish 15 cm / 6 inches in diameter.

Heat the oven to 170°C / 325°F / gas 3.

Cut the brioche loaf into 5-mm / ¹/₄-inch thick slices and trim off the dark crusts. Cut out nine 5.5-cm / 2¹/₄-inch discs; reserve all the trimmings.

Lightly beat the eggs with the remaining sugar. Bring the milk almost to the boil in a heavy-based saucepan. Slowly add to the egg mixture, stirring constantly, and stir until the sugar has dissolved. Strain the egg mixture.

Melt the remaining butter and use to moisten the brioche trimmings and discs. Place half the trimmings evenly over the butter caramel in the soufflé dish. Pour over one-third of the egg mixture and sprinkle over half of the apricots with any soaking liquid. Repeat the layers. Arrange the brioche discs neatly over the top, slightly overlapping. Slowly pour the rest of the egg mixture evenly over the discs, letting them soak it up as you pour. Leave to stand for 5 minutes so the brioche can soak up the custard.

Set the soufflé dish in a roasting pan and add enough hot water to the pan to come halfway up the sides of the dish. Transfer the pan to the oven and bake for 45–55 minutes or until the pudding is just set and lightly browned on top. The water should not boil so reduce the oven temperature slightly if necessary.

Warm the apricot jam in a small pan until melted. If necessary, press the jam through a sieve to remove any pieces of fruit.

Remove the baked pudding from the oven and brush the top with the jam to glaze it. Serve warm.

STEAMED SULTANA PUDDING

Serves 4-6

This is my favourite English winter pudding – I call it a happy man's pudding because you feel very content after eating it.

100 g / 3¹/₂ oz / 7 tbsp unsalted butter, at
   room temperature
100 g / 3¹/₂ oz / ¹/₂ cup caster sugar [US
   granulated sugar]
2 eggs
200 g / 7 oz / 1¹/₃ cups flour

1 tsp baking powder
a pinch of salt
3 tbsp milk
100 g / 3¹/₂ oz / ²/₃ cup sultanas [US golden
   raisins]
Vanilla Custard Sauce (see page 25), to serve

Lightly butter a 1.2-litre / 2-pint / 5-cup pudding basin.

Cream the butter with the sugar until the mixture is light and fluffy. Add the eggs one at a time, beating well. Sift together the flour, baking powder and salt and add to the creamed mixture. Fold in with a rubber spatula. Add the milk and mix it in well. Fold in the sultanas.

Pour the mixture into the pudding basin. Cover the top with a disc of baking parchment, then seal with foil.

Place the basin in the top of a steamer or double boiler over simmering water. Alternatively, put the basin in a heavy-based pan and add boiling water to the pan to come three-quarters of the way up the sides of the basin. Cover and cook for 2 hours, replenishing the water when necessary.

Turn out the pudding on to a warmed serving dish and serve with the vanilla custard sauce.

LIME TART

Serves 10

1/2 quantity Sweet Pastry (see page 26)
4 eggs
300 g / 10 oz / 1 1/2 cups caster sugar
[US granulated sugar]
250 ml / 8 fl oz / 1 cup double cream
[US heavy whipping cream]

finely grated zest of 1 unwaxed lime
200 ml / 7 fl oz / 7/8 cup freshly squeezed
lime juice
4 tsp lemon juice
a drop of natural green food colouring

Heat the oven to 200°C / 400°F / gas 6.

Roll out the pastry dough thinly and use to line a 25-cm / 10-inch diameter loose-based flan tin [US tart pan] or flan ring set on a baking sheet. It is important that the pastry dough be evenly rolled and then pressed gently into the tin so that no holes are made. Line the pastry case with grease-proof paper [US wax paper] and weigh this down with ceramic baking beans or dried beans. Bake for 12 minutes.

Meanwhile, combine the eggs and sugar in a bowl and whisk gently to mix. Mix in the cream. Leave to stand for 10 minutes, then stir the mixture. If there is any froth on the surface, skim it off.

Remove the pastry case from the oven

and discard the beans and paper. Put the pastry case back in the oven for 3–4 minutes to set the base, then remove the case again. Reduce the oven temperature to 170°C / 325°F / gas 3.

Gently stir the lime zest and juice and lemon juice into the cream mixture. Add the green food colouring. Pour the mixture into the pastry case and leave to settle for 2 minutes. Lay a paper towel on the surface of the filling to absorb any remaining froth.

Carefully place the tart in the oven and bake for 40–50 minutes or until the filling is set and the pastry is golden brown. Leave to cool completely before serving.

TIPS

The filling should not be allowed to boil or it will curdle, so if necessary reduce the oven temperature a little. You can also leave the oven door ajar during the final part of baking.

If your oven heats unevenly, you may need to turn the tart during baking so that it cooks evenly.

If the pastry is browning too quickly before the filling has set, cover with foil.

Adding the filling to a hot pastry case speeds up the cooking and ensures that the base of the pastry case isn't soggy.

BLUEBERRY TARTLETS

Makes 4

This is a simple and quick recipe and an absolute delight to eat.

TIP

If the jam glaze is too thick to brush on the berries, stir in a few drops of hot water.

200 g / 7 oz Puff Pastry (see page 27)
4 tbsp Frangipane (see page 155)
120 g / 4 oz / 1 cup fresh blueberries
4 tbsp apricot jam

icing sugar [US confectioners' sugar], to finish
clotted cream or whipped cream, to serve

Roll out the puff pastry to 3-mm / ¹⁄₈-inch thickness. Cut out 4 discs, each 10 cm / 4 inches in diameter. Transfer the discs to a baking sheet and chill for 1 hour.

Heat the oven to 190°C / 375°F / gas 5.

Prick the pastry discs all over with a fork. Divide the frangipane among the discs and spread it evenly to within 3 mm / ¹⁄₈ inch of the edges. Arrange the blueberries on top.

Bake for about 15 minutes or until the pastry is lightly browned and crisp around the edges.

Meanwhile, warm the apricot jam in a small pan until it is liquid. If necessary, press it through a fine sieve to remove any pieces of fruit.

When the tartlets are ready, remove them from the oven and brush the blueberries with the jam glaze. Transfer to serving plates and dust the edge of each plate with sifted icing sugar. Add a scoop of clotted cream or whipped cream to each plate and serve immediately.

BLACK FOREST CHERRY TART

Serves 4-6

You can also make this tart with plums or apricots. Just cut them in half and remove the stones [US pits].

225 g / 8 oz / 1²/₃ cups flour
1 tsp baking powder
¹/₂ tsp salt
120 g / 4 oz / 1 stick (8 tbsp) cold
  unsalted butter
100 g / 3¹/₂ oz / ¹/₂ cup caster sugar
  [US granulated sugar]
finely grated zest of 1 unwaxed lemon
1 egg

500 g / 1 lb 2 oz fresh cherries
a little egg white
200 ml / 7 fl oz / ⁷/₈ cup plain yogurt
shavings of cinnamon stick, to decorate

For serving
Raspberry Sauce (see box)
Cinnamon Ice Cream (see page 177)

Combine the flour, baking powder and salt in a bowl. Cut the butter into cubes and rub into the flour until the mixture is like crumbs. Add all but 1 tbsp of the sugar, the lemon zest and egg and mix together to form a dough. Wrap and chill for 1 hour.

Roll out two-thirds of the dough to 5-mm / ¹/₄-inch thickness and use to line a buttered 15-cm / 6-inch diameter flan ring placed on a baking sheet. You could also use a loose-bottomed flan tin [US tart pan].

Wash and dry the cherries, then remove the stones [US pits]. Pack the cherries tightly in the tart case and press them firmly into the dough.

Roll out the remaining dough to a round 5 mm / ¹/₄ inch thick. Lay it over the cherries. Cut off excess dough, then press the edges gently down inside the ring to seal. Chill for 20 minutes.

Heat the oven to 190°C / 375°F / gas 5.

Brush the top with egg white and sprinkle with the reserved sugar. Bake the tart for 25–30 minutes or until the pastry is golden brown. Allow it to cool slightly, then remove the flan ring or side of the pan. Cut the tart into neat wedges.

Make a small pool of yogurt on each plate, just off-centre, and surround with a ring of raspberry sauce. Feather the two together using a wooden cocktail stick or skewer. Place a piece of tart on the edge of the sauce.

To shape the ice cream, dip a dessert-spoon in hot water, then scrape it across the surface of the ice cream, rolling it into the spoon to make a neat shape. Place the ice cream next to the pieces of tart. Decorate the ice cream with shavings of cinnamon and serve.

RIGHT
Black Forest Cherry Tart

RASPBERRY SAUCE
This excellent sauce can be served with many desserts. In our healthy lives nowadays, it is ideal to use in place of cream. Purée 300 g / 10 oz / 2¹/₂ cups raspberries with 2 tsp lemon juice and 45 g / 1¹/₂ oz / 6 tbsp icing sugar [US confectioners' sugar] in a blender or food processor. Press the sauce through a fine sieve to remove the raspberry seeds. Makes about 300 ml / ¹/₂ pint / 1¹/₄ cups.

POACHED PEACHES WITH MASCARPONE AND ALMONDS

Serves 4

400 g / 14 oz / 2 cups sugar
1 vanilla pod [US vanilla bean]
4 large, ripe but firm peaches
30 g / 1 oz / 2 tbsp mascarpone cheese
100 g / 3 1/2 oz / 1 cup flaked almonds
   [US sliced almonds]

For the mascarpone sabayon
125 ml / 4 fl oz / 1/2 cup double cream
   [US heavy whipping cream]
120 g / 4 oz / 1/2 cup mascarpone cheese
3 tbsp peach brandy, schnapps or fruit eau de vie
1 tsp lemon juice
2 egg yolks
45 g / 1 1/2 oz / 1/4 cup caster sugar
   [US granulated sugar]

Combine the sugar and 500 ml / 16 fl oz / 2 cups water in a deep saucepan. Split the vanilla pod open and add to the pan. Heat, stirring, to dissolve the sugar, then bring to the boil and simmer for 1 minute.

Cut a cross in the skin at the base of each peach. Add the peaches to the syrup and poach for 10 seconds. Lift them out with a slotted spoon and immerse in iced water. When they are cool enough to handle, slip off their skins.

Return the peeled peaches to the syrup and poach until they are just tender – 5 minutes or so, according to ripeness. Drain. When the peaches are cool enough to handle, push out the stones [US pits] without splitting open the peaches: make a little incision at the stalk end, then insert a chopstick or end of a wooden spoon handle into the other side and push out the stone through the incision. Cover and chill for 30 minutes.

Put the mascarpone in a small piping bag [US pastry bag] or paper piping cone and pipe into each peach to fill the hollow left by the stone. Arrange the peaches in a flameproof serving dish and chill until ready to finish for serving.

Heat the grill [US broiler]. Toast the almonds under the grill, shaking the pan so they colour evenly. Set them aside.

To make the sabayon, whip the cream until it is beginning to thicken. Add the mascarpone and continue whipping until the mixture is thick but not stiff. Set aside.

Put the brandy and lemon juice in a small pan and bring to the boil.

Combine the egg yolks and sugar in a large heatproof bowl and set over a pan of gently simmering water. Beat or whisk until the mixture is pale and thick and well increased in volume.

Remove the bowl from the pan of water and whisk in the brandy mixture. Continue whisking until the mixture is cold. Fold the mascarpone cream gently but thoroughly into the whisked mixture.

Cover the peaches with the mascarpone sabayon and sprinkle the toasted almonds on top. Grill close to the heat just until the surface is glazed and lightly coloured. Serve immediately.

PEAR TATIN WITH
POIRE WILLIAMS SAUCE

Serves 4-6

TIP
Warm the base of the dish over very low heat or in a moderate oven before turning out the Tatin. This will make it easier to unmould.

Japanese Nashi pears have a very firm, crisp texture and wonderful flavour that is a cross between apple and pear.

*150 g / 5 oz / ³/4 cup caster sugar
[US granulated sugar]*
¹/2 tsp liquid glucose [US light corn syrup]
100 g / 3¹/2 oz / 7 tbsp unsalted butter

*6 Nashi or other Japanese or Chinese pears
120 g / 4 oz Puff Pastry (see page 27)
icing sugar [US confectioners' sugar], to finish
Poire Williams Sauce (see box), to serve*

Heat a heavy-based saucepan over moderate heat. Put in 120 g / 4 oz / 10 tbsp of the caster sugar and melt it, stirring often, then cook until it caramelizes to a rich brown. Stir in the glucose and 60 g / 2 oz / 4 tbsp of the butter, a little at a time.

Pour the butter caramel into a 20-cm / 8-inch round baking dish that is 4 cm / 1¹/2 inches deep. Leave to cool; the butter caramel should then have a firm but not hard consistency.

Peel, halve and core the pears, then slice them thinly. Place half of them on the butter caramel, to fill the dish. Bake for

about 25 minutes or until the pear slices are translucent and have reduced in volume by about half.

Meanwhile, melt the remaining butter in a frying pan over low heat. Add the remaining pear slices and sprinkle with the remaining sugar. Cover and cook gently for 10–12 minutes or until the slices are tender. Drain.

Arrange the cooked pear slices on top of the pears in the baking dish and press down firmly. Set aside to cool.

Roll out the puff pastry about 3 mm / ¹/8 inch thick and cut a round large enough to cover the dish. Prick the surface all over with a fork. Leave to rest for 20 minutes.

Heat the oven to 200°C / 400°F / gas 6.

Place the pastry round on top of the pears and press down gently. Bake for about 20 minutes or until the pastry is golden brown.

Heat the grill [US broiler].

Dust the pastry with sifted icing sugar and glaze under the grill. Leave to cool, then set aside for 2 hours.

Turn out the Tatin on to a serving dish so the pastry is on the bottom. Serve at room temperature, with the warm sauce.

POIRE WILLIAMS SAUCE

This sauce is also wonderful with all kinds of apple desserts, from baked apples to apple crumble or apple crisp, as well as with ice cream. Warm a heavy-based saucepan over moderate heat. Combine 200 g / 7 oz / 1 cup sugar, 4 tbsp water and 1 tbsp liquid glucose [US light corn syrup] in the saucepan. Bring to the boil, stirring to dissolve the sugar, then boil gently until the syrup turns a light caramel colour. Remove from the heat and add 200 g / 7 oz / 14 tbsp unsalted butter, a little at a time. Stir in 200 ml / 7 fl oz / ⁷/8 cup double cream [US heavy whipping cream], then add 4 tbsp Poire Williams liqueur. Strain the sauce through a fine sieve, and serve it warm. Makes about 400 ml / 14 fl oz / 1³/4 cups.

PEARS IN PUFF PASTRY WITH VANILLA ICE CREAM AND CHOCOLATE SAUCE

Serves 4

400 g / 14 oz / 2 cups sugar
1 vanilla pod [US vanilla bean]
4 large dessert pears
300 g / 10 oz good-quality plain chocolate
  [US bittersweet chocolate]
225 g / 8 oz Puff Pastry (see page 27)

1 egg yolk
Vanilla Ice Cream (see page 177), to serve
100 ml / 3 1/2 fl oz / 7 tbsp double cream
  [US heavy whipping cream]
fresh mint leaves, to decorate

Combine the sugar and split-open vanilla pod in a deep saucepan. Add 500 ml / 16 fl oz / 2 cups water and bring to the boil, stirring to dissolve the sugar.

Meanwhile, peel the pears and trim off the tops of the stalks with scissors. Using a melon baller or small knife, cut out the cores, working from the blossom or wide end of each pear, to create a cavity. If necessary, cut a very thin slice from the base of each pear so it will stand upright.

Add the pears to the sugar syrup and poach until they are just tender – 6 minutes or so, according to ripeness. Drain the pears and set aside to cool.

Break the chocolate into a heatproof bowl or into the top of a double boiler. Set over a pan of simmering water and stir the chocolate until it is melted and smooth. Remove from the heat.

Set each pear stalk end down in a narrow cup or glass. Pour enough melted chocolate into the cavity to fill it. Refrigerate until the chocolate has set.

Roll out the puff pastry to a rough rectangle 3 mm / 1/8 inch thick. Cut it into quarters, each quarter large enough to enclose a pear. Lightly beat the egg yolk with 1/2 tsp water. Wrap each pear tightly in pastry, brushing all the joins with the egg wash and pressing to seal. Trim the pastry at the top and twist it slightly to make a stalk shape. Trim the edges at the base to neaten them, then tuck them under and press to seal the base well so no chocolate can escape.

Brush the pastry-wrapped pears all over with the egg wash and arrange on a small baking sheet. Leave to rest in the refrigerator for at least 20 minutes.

Heat the oven to 200°C / 400°F / gas 6.

Brush the pastry-wrapped pears with egg wash again. Bake for about 20 minutes or until the pastry is puffed and golden brown.

Meanwhile, put a scoop of vanilla ice cream in the centre of each chilled plate and spread it out into a flat disc about 1 cm / 1/2 inch thick. Keep in the freezer until ready to serve.

Warm the remaining chocolate very gently to melt it again and stir in the cream. Heat until the sauce is shiny and smooth.

Set a hot pear on each ice cream disc, garnish with a mint leaf and serve immediately, with the warm chocolate sauce.

TIP

The higher the content of cocoa (cocoa solids and cocoa butter) in chocolate, the more depth of flavour it will have. Ideally the cocoa content should be 35% or more. In choosing chocolate to use in the recipes in this book, please check the cocoa content on the label. [A note for US cooks: bittersweet chocolate contains at least 35% chocolate liquor, whereas semisweet chocolate contains 15–35%.]

PINEAPPLE WONTONS

Serves 4

These are folded into the shape of a 3-pointed crown. The pineapple and apricot filling is spiced with freshly crushed cloves.

1 ripe pineapple, weighing about 450 g / 1 lb
  without the leaves
5 whole cloves
3 pieces of stem ginger in syrup
60 g / 2 oz / 3 tbsp apricot jam
20 wonton wrappers [US wonton skins], each
  about 7.5 cm / 3 inches square
½ egg white
vegetable oil for deep frying

To finish
icing sugar [US confectioners' sugar]
Prune Sorbet (see page 180) or Banana and
  Honey Sorbet (see page 180)
fresh mint leaves

Peel the pineapple, removing all the 'eyes'. Cut it lengthwise into quarters and cut away the core, then chop the flesh into very small dice. Drain the flesh to remove all excess juice. Finely crush the cloves with a mortar and pestle. Drain and finely dice the ginger.

Put the apricot jam in a saucepan and heat until melted. Stir in the pineapple, cloves and ginger. Remove from the heat and leave to cool.

Lay the wonton wrappers out flat. Put ½ tsp of the pineapple mixture in the centre of each one. Lightly beat the egg white. Brush the edges of each wonton lightly with egg white, then fold over into a triangle and press the edges together to seal. Fold the two outside points up and in to make the 3-pointed crown shape. Brush with a little egg white and press to seal.

Heat oil for deep frying to 170°C / 325°F.

Fry the wontons for about 1½ minutes or until golden brown on both sides. Drain on paper towels.

Arrange the wontons on the warmed plates and add a spoonful of the remaining pineapple mixture to each plate. Dust the edge of each plate with sifted icing sugar. Add a spoonful of sorbet to each serving, garnish with a mint leaf and serve.

CHOCOLATE GÂTEAU WITH GRAND MARNIER

Serves 6

1 Sponge Cake (see page 28)
2 tbsp apricot jam
125 ml / 4 fl oz / 1/2 cup orange juice
5 tbsp Grand Marnier
2 leaves of gelatine
350 g / 12 oz good-quality milk chocolate
300 ml / 1/2 pint / 1 1/4 cups double cream
 [US heavy whipping cream]
1 tbsp ground hazelnuts

For the shortbread base
70 g / scant 2 1/2 oz / 1/2 cup flour
30 g / 2 oz / 2 1/2 tbsp caster sugar
 [US superfine sugar]
40 g / scant 1 1/2 oz / 3 tbsp unsalted butter,
 at room temperature
1 egg yolk

TIP
Just before serving, carefully lift off the flan ring and peel away the paper.

Line a baking sheet with baking parchment [US nonstick silicone paper].

First make the shortbread base. Combine the flour, sugar and butter in a bowl and rub together to a fine crumb. Bind to a dough with the egg yolk. Put the dough on the paper-lined baking sheet and press it out to a neat round about 5 mm / 1/4 inch thick and 17.5 cm / 7 inches in diameter. Prick the surface all over with a fork. Chill for 15 minutes.

Heat the oven to 180°C / 350°F / gas 4.

Bake the shortbread round for about 12 minutes or until golden brown. Leave to cool on a wire rack.

Cut a 5-mm / 1/4-inch thick layer from the sponge cake and reserve. Keep the remainder of the cake for another recipe.

Line a cold baking sheet with baking parchment. Put the shortbread base on the parchment. Warm the apricot jam until melted, then if necessary press it through a fine sieve to remove bits of fruit. Spread it evenly over the shortbread. Set the sponge cake layer on top and press gently together. Line an 18.5-cm / 7 1/2-inch flan ring that is 5 cm / 2 inches deep with parchment. Place it on the baking sheet, around the shortbread and cake.

Using a pastry brush, moisten the cake with half of the orange juice and 1 1/2 tbsp of the Grand Marnier.

Soak the gelatine leaves in 3 1/2 tbsp cold water until softened. Drain the gelatine and squeeze out excess water, then return it to the bowl. Add the remaining orange juice and Grand Marnier. Set the bowl in a pan of simmering water and stir to melt the gelatine. Do not let the mixture boil.

Break the chocolate into a heatproof bowl or into the top of a double boiler. Set over a pan of simmering water and stir the chocolate until it is melted and smooth. Remove from the heat and cool slightly. Add the Grand Marnier mixture. Whip the cream until thick but not stiff. Add the chocolate mixture and stir to a smooth, velvety consistency.

Pour the chocolate mixture slowly around the rim of the cake, inside the flan ring, so it runs down the sides into the gap between the cake and the flan ring, then pour on to the centre of the cake and smooth the top. Put the hazelnuts in a coarse sieve and rub through to dust the surface of the chocolate cream.

Cover and chill for about 1 1/2 hours or until the chocolate cream has set.

VANILLA ICE CREAM

Makes about 1 litre / 1³/4 pints / 1 US quart

This ice cream cannot be softened for serving and then refrozen.

500 ml / 16 fl oz / 2 cups cold Vanilla Custard Sauce (see page 25)

500 ml / 16 fl oz / 2 cups double cream [US heavy whipping cream]

Combine the custard sauce and cream in a large freezerproof bowl. Cover and freeze for 2 hours or until it begins to firm up.

Transfer the half-frozen ice cream to a blender or food processor and whizz until it is creamy and the ice crystals are broken down. Pour back into the bowl, cover and return to the freezer. Freeze until it firms up again, then whizz in the blender or food processor as before. Cover and freeze again, whizzing one more time, then freeze until firm. The ice cream is now ready for serving.

If the ice cream is left in the freezer and has frozen very hard, transfer it to the refrigerator 20–30 minutes before serving so that it can soften slightly.

Variations

CINNAMON ICE CREAM: Combine 1 litre / 1³/4 pints / 1 quart double cream [US heavy whipping cream] and 2¹/2 very fresh cinnamon sticks in a saucepan. Bring to the boil and boil until reduced by half. Strain the cream and allow to cool. Use this cinnamon-scented cream with 500 ml / 16 fl oz / 2 cups Vanilla Custard Sauce to make the ice cream, as instructed above.

MASCARPONE ICE CREAM: Use 250 ml / 8 fl oz / 1 cup Vanilla Custard Sauce and 125 ml / 4 fl oz / ¹/2 cup double cream [US heavy whipping cream]. Add 225 g / 8 oz mascarpone cheese and mix well until smooth (a hand blender is ideal for this). Freeze as above. After the final whizzing in the food processor, mix in 4 tsp maraschino liqueur and 30 g / 1 oz / 3 tbsp finely chopped pistachio nuts.

SUMMER TEASER

Serves 4

juice of 3 limes
150 ml / 1/4 pint / 2/3 cup Chablis or other
  dry white wine
4 tbsp crème de cassis (blackcurrant liqueur)
60 g / 2 oz / 1/2 cup icing sugar
  [US confectioners' sugar]

2 tsp chopped fresh mint
350 g / 12 oz mixed summer berries such as
  raspberries, strawberries, blackberries, wild
  strawberries, blueberries and loganberries
Strawberry Sorbet (see below), to serve
fresh mint, to decorate

Mix together the lime juice, white wine and crème de cassis. Sift in the sugar and whisk well to mix. Stir in the chopped mint. Cover and chill for at least 1 hour.

Rinse the berries and dry them carefully. Divide them among serving dishes such as small soup plates. Strain the lime mixture and spoon it over the berries.

To shape the sorbet, dip a dessertspoon in hot water, then scrape it across the surface of the sorbet, rolling the sorbet into the spoon to make a neat shape. Put the sorbet on top of the berries, add a sprig of mint and serve.

TIPS

For this light and refreshing dessert, you can use any soft fruit in season and other flavours of sorbet or ice cream.

On a hot day, the macerated berries, without the sorbet, make an excellent first course.

STRAWBERRY SORBET

Serves 6

350 g / 12 oz / 1 pint ripe red strawberries
juice of 1 lemon

60 g / 2 oz / 5 tbsp sugar

Remove hulls from the strawberries, then wash and dry them. Purée the strawberries with the lemon juice in a blender or food processor.

Combine the sugar and 6 tbsp water in a saucepan and bring to the boil, stirring to dissolve the sugar. Remove from the heat and set aside to cool completely. Stir in the strawberry purée.

Freeze the mixture in an ice cream machine or sorbetière, according to the manufacturer's instructions.

Alternatively, pour the mixture into a

large freezerproof bowl, cover and freeze until almost set. Transfer to a food processor and whizz until broken up and well mixed. Return to the bowl, cover and freeze for 3 hours or until almost set, then whizz in the food processor again. Cover and freeze for 2 hours. Just before serving, mash the sorbet well with a fork.

If the sorbet is left in the freezer and has frozen very hard, transfer it to the refrigerator 20–30 minutes before serving so that it can soften slightly.

TIP

Ideally, this sorbet – and all others – should be served as soon as it is ready because the flavour will diminish if it is kept in the freezer for very long.

RIGHT
Summer Teaser

BANANA AND HONEY SORBET

Serves 6

600 g / 1 1/4 lb ripe bananas
100 g / 3 1/2 oz / 1/3 cup honey

3 1/2 tbsp sugar

Peel the bananas; there should be 400 g / 14 oz net weight. Purée them in a blender or food processor. [US cooks should measure 1 3/4 cups banana purée.]

Combine the honey, sugar and 100 ml / 3 1/2 fl oz / 7 tbsp of water in a saucepan and bring slowly to the boil, stirring to dissolve the sugar. Add this syrup to the bananas and mix well. Leave to cool.

Freeze the mixture in an ice cream machine or sorbetière, according to the manufacturer's instructions.

Alternatively, pour the mixture into a large freezerproof bowl, cover and freeze until almost set. Transfer to a food processor and whizz until broken up and well mixed. Return to the bowl, cover and freeze for 2 hours or until almost set. Using a fork, mash the sorbet well to break it up. Cover and freeze again for 1 hour. Just before serving, mash the sorbet once more.

If the sorbet is left in the freezer and has frozen very hard, transfer it to the refrigerator 20–30 minutes before serving.

TIP

A flower honey is best for this. I like orange blossom honey best.

PRUNE SORBET

Serves 6

250 g / 9 oz pitted prunes
juice of 1 1/2 lemons

1/2 cinnamon stick
2 tbsp sugar

Put the prunes in a bowl, cover with water and leave to soak overnight.

Drain the prunes. Finely chop 6 of them and reserve. Put the remaining prunes in a food processor with 100 ml /3 1/2 fl oz / 7 tbsp of water and process until roughly chopped but not a purée.

Combine the lemon juice, cinnamon stick and 300 ml / 1/2 pint / 1 1/4 cups of water in a saucepan and bring to the boil. Add the sugar and stir until it has dissolved. Stir in the prune mixture from the food processor. Remove from the heat and leave to cool completely. Discard the cinnamon.

Freeze the mixture in an ice cream machine or sorbetière, according to manufacturer's instructions. Stir in the reserved prunes when the sorbet is half set.

Alternatively, pour the mixture into a large freezerproof bowl, cover and freeze until almost set. Using a fork, mash the sorbet well to break it up. Cover and return to the freezer. Freeze for 2 hours, then mash with a fork as before. Mix in the reserved chopped prunes. Cover and freeze again for 1 hour. Just before serving, mash the sorbet once more.

If the sorbet is left in the freezer and has frozen very hard, transfer it to the refrigerator 20–30 minutes before serving.

FROZEN AMARETTO SOUFFLÉ

Makes 5

150 ml / ¹/₄ pint / ²/₃ cup double cream
   [US heavy whipping cream]
16 amaretto biscuits [US amaretto cookies]
2 tbsp Amaretto di Saronno liqueur
4 egg yolks

6¹/₂ tbsp caster sugar [US granulated sugar]
120 g / 4 oz good-quality plain chocolate
   [US bittersweet chocolate]
1¹/₂ tbsp sunflower oil
tiny sprigs of fresh mint, to decorate

Whip the cream until it is thick but not stiff. Crumble 12 of the amaretto biscuits into another bowl and sprinkle them with the liqueur.

Combine the egg yolks and sugar in a large heatproof bowl and set over a pan of gently simmering water. Beat or whisk until the mixture is pale and thick and well increased in volume. Remove the bowl from the pan of water and continue to whisk until the mixture is lukewarm.

Reserve 2 tbsp of the whipped cream. Fold the remainder into the egg yolk mixture. Fold in the soaked amaretto biscuits.

Spoon the mixture into 5 straight-sided freezerproof moulds, 125 ml / 4 fl oz / ¹/₂ cup capacity, filling them to the top. Smooth the tops, then cover and freeze for about 6 hours or until firm.

Break the chocolate into a heatproof bowl or into the top of a double boiler. Set over a pan of simmering water and stir the chocolate until it is melted and smooth. Remove from the heat and stir in the sunflower oil. Set aside until cool but still liquid.

Dip each mould briefly in hot water, then turn out the frozen soufflés. Return them to the freezer for a few minutes to harden them. Dip the soufflés into the melted chocolate so they are half coated. Set them on a sheet of greaseproof paper [US wax paper].

Put the reserved whipped cream in a paper piping cone and pipe a rosette on each frozen soufflé. Decorate with a whole amaretto biscuit and a tiny mint sprig, and serve immediately.

TIPS

To make unmoulding and dipping very easy, insert a wooden ice-lolly stick [US popsicle stick] in the centre of each soufflé before freezing.

At The Savoy, we use demitasse cups to mould these frozen soufflés.

Once the soufflés have been dipped in chocolate, they can be returned to the freezer and kept for a day or so before serving.

You can make these soufflés with any other flavour you like, such as Grand Marnier, crème de menthe, cherry brandy, etc. Replace the amaretto biscuits with sponge cake (see recipe on page 28).

THEO'S FRUIT CAKE

Makes a loaf-shaped cake that cuts into about 16 slices

Theo is one of the pastry chefs at The Savoy. He developed this very light and spicy fruit cake, which makes a nice change from the traditional, heavy type. You can bake it in any shape of tin you like.

soft unsalted butter for the pan
150 g / 5 oz / 10 tbsp unsalted butter, at
* room temperature*
125 g / 4¹/₂ oz / ³/₄ cup demerara sugar
* [US raw brown sugar]*
4 eggs, size 2 [US extra large]
200 g / 7 oz / 1¹/₃ cups flour
4 tsp baking powder
1 tsp ground cinnamon

1 tsp mixed spice [US apple pie spice]
45 g / 1¹/₂ oz / ¹/₃ cup walnut pieces
90 g / 3 oz / ¹/₂ cup glacé cherries
* [US candied cherries]*
75 g / 2¹/₂ oz candied orange peel
75 g / 2¹/₂ oz candied lemon peel
30 g / 1 oz candied angelica
150 g / 5 oz / 1 cup raisins

Heat the oven to 170°C / 325°F / gas 3. Grease a 900-g / 2-lb loaf pan that measures about 23 x 12.5 x 7.5 cm / 9 x 5 x 3 inches, then line it with greaseproof paper [US wax paper].

With an electric mixer at high speed, cream the butter with the sugar until pale and fluffy. Lightly beat the eggs with a fork, then gradually beat half into the creamed mixture at medium speed. Sift together the flour, baking powder and spices. Add half to the creamed mixture, then beat in the remaining beaten egg followed by the remaining flour.

Coarsely chop the walnuts. Cut the cherries in half. Dice the orange and lemon peels and the angelica. Add the walnuts, cherries, candied peel, angelica and raisins to the cake batter and fold them in gently and evenly. Pour the batter into the prepared loaf pan.

Bake for 1–1¹/₄ hours or until the cake is lightly browned on top and a skewer inserted into the centre comes out clean. If the surface is browning too much towards the end of baking, cover the cake with foil.

Leave to cool in the pan.

TIP
When adding beaten egg to creamed butter and sugar, the mixture might curdle. But don't worry. Just add 1–2 tbsp of the measured flour and continue beating in the remaining egg. If the mixture still has a curdled appearance after all the egg has been added, you can set the base of the bowl in another bowl of hot water, then beat briskly. Once all the flour has been added, the mixture will no doubt be smooth.

RIGHT
Theo's Fruit Cake

CHRISTMAS STOLLEN

Makes 1 loaf

This recipe takes me back to my childhood, and the annual ritual in November when my mother made the stollens for Christmas. The time until Christmas, when you could finally eat the stollen, seemed endless.

100 ml / 3¹/₂ fl oz / 7 tbsp milk
1 vanilla pod [US vanilla bean]
15 g / ¹/₂ oz fresh yeast
250 g / 8¹/₂ oz / 1³/₄ cups flour
3 tbsp caster sugar [US granulated sugar]
a pinch of salt
2 egg yolks
100 g / 3¹/₂ oz / 7 tbsp unsalted butter
100 g / 3¹/₂ oz / ²/₃ cup raisins
45 g / 1¹/₂ oz / ¹/₃ cup chopped mixed
   candied peel

finely grated zest and juice of 1 unwaxed
   lemon
1 tbsp dark rum
35 g / 1¹/₄ oz / ¹/₄ cup whole blanched
   almonds
60 g / 2 oz hazelnut marzipan (optional)

To finish
melted unsalted butter
caster or icing sugar [US granulated or
   confectioners' sugar]

Warm the milk in a pan with the split-open vanilla pod. Cover and set aside to infuse for 20 minutes.

Remove and discard the vanilla pod. Warm the milk to lukewarm again and pour it into a bowl. Add the yeast and mash with a spoon until creamy. Leave in a warm place for 10 minutes.

Sift the flour, sugar and salt into a large bowl. Add the yeast mixture and egg yolks and mix to a dough. Knead for 5 minutes or until smooth. Cut the butter into pieces and scatter over the surface of the dough. Cover the bowl with a damp cloth and set aside in a warm place to rise for 2–2¹/₂ hours or until doubled in bulk.

Meanwhile, combine the raisins, candied peel, lemon zest and juice, and rum in a bowl. Set aside to macerate. Toast the almonds (see page 84).

Knead the risen dough gently, mixing in the butter completely. Add the drained fruit and toasted almonds and knead in

until evenly distributed. Cover the bowl again and refrigerate the dough for at least 4 hours or overnight.

Turn the dough on to a cool floured surface. Using a floured rolling pin, roll out the dough to an oblong about 17.5 x 12.5 cm / 7 x 5 inches. The oblong should be 2 cm / ³/₄ inch thick at one end and 4 cm / 1 ¹/₂ inches thick at the other end, with a dip in the centre. Transfer it to a baking sheet.

If using marzipan, shape it into a log about 10 cm / 4 inches long and 2.5 cm / 1 inch in diameter. Put the marzipan log across the thick end of the oblong, where it rises up.

To shape the stollen, fold both thick and thin ends over to meet in the centre, then fold the thick side over again so that it almost completely covers the thin side. The shaped stollen should resemble a fist or snail shell when viewed from the side. Cover and set aside in a warm place to rise

TIPS

Sifting dry ingredients together removes any lumps and aerates the mixture as well as mixing small amounts of raising agents and seasonings evenly throughout.

The dough is rested in the refrigerator because it is easier to shape a cold, unelastic dough.

again for up to 3 hours or until it doubles in bulk.

Heat the oven to 200°C / 400°F / gas 6.

Bake the stollen for about 50 minutes or until it is golden brown. Brush it with melted butter and roll in caster sugar or dust with sifted icing sugar. Leave to cool on a wire rack.

Wrap the stollen in greaseproof paper [US wax paper] and then in foil and place in an airtight container. Allow to mature for 2 weeks before serving.

BANANA BREAD

Makes a loaf-shaped bread that cuts into about 16 slices

soft unsalted butter and flour for the pan
450 g / 1 lb very ripe bananas
225 g / 8 oz / 1 cup + 2 tbsp caster sugar
  [US granulated sugar]
3 eggs

2 tbsp milk
2 tbsp walnut oil
225 g / 8 oz / 1²/₃ cups flour
2 tsp baking powder
100 g / 3¹/₂ oz / 1 cup walnut pieces

Heat the oven to 170°C / 325°F / gas 3. Butter and flour a 900-g / 2-lb loaf pan that measures about 23 x 12.5 x 7.5 cm / 9 x 5 x 3 inches.

Peel the bananas; there should be 300 g / 10 oz net weight. Put them in a bowl and mash with a fork. [US cooks should measure 1¹/₄ cups mashed bananas.] Add the sugar and mash in well. Lightly beat the eggs with the milk. Gradually mix into the bananas. Stir in the walnut oil. Sift the flour with the baking powder and stir into the mixture. Coarsely chop the walnuts and mix them in.

Turn the batter into the prepared pan. Bake for 1–1¹/₄ hours or until a skewer inserted into the centre comes out clean.

Turn out of the pan on to a wire rack and leave to cool before serving.

FLAMBÉED GOAT'S CHEESE WITH ARMAGNAC AND GARLIC CROÛTES

Serves 4

This is one of the most exciting ways to eat goat's cheese. It becomes very moist and crumbly when heated, and the sharpness almost completely disappears, leaving a rich and nutty flavour. You could also serve this as a snack or as a light meal.

2 round Crottin de Chavignol or 4 slices of
  another firm goat's cheese, each 2 cm /
  3/4 inch thick
200 ml / 7 fl oz / 7/8 cup olive oil
1 garlic clove
a few sprigs each of fresh thyme, rosemary
  and sage
45 g / 1 1/2 oz / 3 tbsp soft butter

100 ml / 3 1/2 fl oz / 7 tbsp double cream
  [US heavy whipping cream]
1/2 loaf of French bread (baguette)
2 handfuls of lamb's lettuce (mâche)
1 apple
2 tbsp Sherry Vinaigrette (see page 21)
freshly ground black pepper
2 tbsp Armagnac

If using Crottin de Chavignol, cut each one horizontally in half to make 2 discs.

Combine the olive oil, peeled garlic clove and herbs in a deep bowl or jar. Add the goat's cheese. Cover and refrigerate overnight.

Remove the cheese from the oil and dry on paper towels. Remove the garlic from the oil and chop it to a paste (see page 13). Mix the garlic with the butter.

Heat the grill [US broiler].

Put the cream in a small pan and boil to reduce to about 2 tbsp. Cut the French bread into 5-mm / 1/4-inch slices. Spread the slices very thinly on both sides with the garlic butter and arrange on the grill pan. Toast under the grill until golden brown on both sides. Keep warm.

Meanwhile, pick apart the lamb's lettuce, then wash and dry it. Peel and core the apple and cut into small dice. Toss the lamb's lettuce and apple with the vinaigrette and season with pepper.

Arrange the slices of goat's cheese on the grill pan and top each with 1/2 tbsp of the reduced cream. Grill for about 3 minutes or until the cheese is soft and lightly browned on top. Remove from the heat.

Warm the Armagnac in a small pan or ladle. Set it alight with a match and pour it, flaming, over the cheese. When the flames have died away, place a slice of cheese in the centre of each plate and spoon over the Armagnac. Arrange the apples and lamb's lettuce around the cheese. Serve with the garlic croûtes.

TIP
You can keep the goat's cheese in the jar of oil, in the refrigerator, for several weeks.

RIGHT
Flambéed Goat's Cheese with Armagnac and Garlic Croûtes

MARINATED RÉBLOCHON WITH RADISHES

Serves 4

120 g / 4 oz mooli [US daikon]
salt and freshly ground black pepper
120 g / 4 oz red radishes
1 large Réblochon, weighing about 180 g / 6 oz
dark peasant bread, to serve

For the marinade
1 tbsp white wine vinegar
3 tbsp extra virgin olive oil
1 tbsp finely chopped shallots
3 tbsp chopped fresh chives
1 tsp caraway seeds
1/2 tsp paprika

TIP
Other cheeses can be prepared in this way. Münster is particularly good.

Peel the mooli. Cut it lengthwise in half, then slice across very thinly. Sprinkle the mooli with salt and set aside to drain for 10 minutes.

Meanwhile, top and tail the radishes, cut them in half and then slice thinly. Remove the rind from the cheese and cut it into cubes about 2-cm / 3/4-inch square. Mix together all the marinade ingredients with 1 tbsp water.

Squeeze the mooli to remove excess moisture. Put it in a bowl and add the red radishes, cubes of cheese and the marinade. Season with salt and pepper. Mix together well, then leave to marinate for at least 10 minutes, tossing occasionally.

Serve at room temperature, with dark peasant bread.

INDEX